INTRODUCTION TO

Financial Math

using the HP-12C calculator

by Dr. Norman Toy

Edited by Alastair Matchett

ADKINS MATCHETT &TOY

NEW YORK   LONDON

Cover design:	Loraine Machlin
Illustrations and cover art:	Jacque Auger
Photo credit:	Robert D. Nelson
Proofreaders:	Karen Lynch
	Jill Stockwell
	Kathleen Adkins

> *Dedicated to Sandy, Michael, and Jonathan*
> *– NET*

Toll-free order line: 1(888) 414-0999

Visit us at www.amttraining.com

www.crunchthenumbers.com

www.directtesting.com

New York 235 Eastern Avenue, Ossining, NY 10562, 1 (914) 944-0999

London   43 Marchmont Street, London WC1N 1AP, +44 20 7916-7030

ABOUT THIS BOOK

It gives you your financial foundation	Financial math is the bedrock of a financial analyst's skill set. You ***have*** to know how to use it!
It has the math you need for finance	This book takes you from ground zero to understanding how math is applied in the capital markets and in corporate finance.
It's self-paced	Move at your own pace. Go straight to the Due Diligence tests if you already know a section. Take the Underwriting test at the end of the book as a final check.

HOW TO USE THIS BOOK

If you...	
Haven't done math in a long time...start here	**Appendices: Algebra brushup and HP calculator intro** ◆ Basic algebra concepts, with practice exercises; an introduction to the HP calculator. ◆ Then go through the entire book.
Have a good understanding of algebra	**Start at the beginning and go straight through** ◆ *Do the exercises, the Due Diligence tests, and the final Underwriting test.*
Have experience in financial math	**Check your mastery of each concept** ◆ *Go to the Due Diligence test in each section and see how well you do. If you don't score at least 80%, review the section.* ◆ *Then complete the Underwriting test.*

INTRO: HOW DEALS GET DONE

Preparation	You gather information, do your homework, and put a proposal together.
The pitch	You pitch your proposal to the client.
The mandate	If the client likes your deal, you get a mandate to proceed.
Hit the phones	The sales force heads for the phones to get indications of interest in a new issue of securities. They have about a minute of an investor's attention to summarize the key points of the deal.
Due Diligence	A check to verify that the deal parties have actually represented the facts accurately.
The underwriting	The underwriting marks the beginning of the actual sale of securities. You'll see a tombstone (announcement) in the papers, and if you worked on the deal, you'll get a copy of the tombstone embedded in plastic to display on your desk. These are the trophies of the capital markets world.

THE BOOK IS SET UP LIKE A DEAL

This book is set up like a deal. You'll do your preparation (the exercises), you'll make a pitch (test your knowledge), accept a mandate (do another test), and hit the phones (get a summary of key points).

Periodically you'll do a check of your understanding (due diligence test).

At the end of the book you can get your underwriting by taking a review test of all the material. If you complete the underwriting successfully, you'll know your math skills are ready for the financial world.

CONTENTS

1. THE CAPITAL MARKETS

INTRODUCTION

> Capital market customers:
> *Savers* and
> *Capital users*

Who uses the capital markets?

The capital markets serve two types of customers:

- ■ **Those who want to save or invest money;**
- ■ **Those who want to raise money or use capital.**

An individual can be both a saver and a user of capital at the same time. For instance, as a saver, I have some money in my checking and savings account, but as a user of capital I have an automobile loan and a home mortgage.

> Intermediaries:
> the go-betweens

Who are the major players in the capital markets?

The capital markets are very large and can be pretty scary to an individual investor or borrower, or to even a company or governmental unit. Institutions who help savers and capital users access the capital markets are called **intermediaries.** Their main role is to match savers and capital users in the most appropriate way.

Intermediaries help savers by combining lots of bite-size investment opportunities, such as deposit accounts, and exploiting economies of scale in investing. They help capital users by packaging together many small funding requirements, such as automobile loans, and exploiting economies of scale in lending. Most customers in the capital markets operate first as savers, depositing money regularly over a long period of time, and later as capital users by withdrawing the money.

An Aunt Millie

An unsophisticated investor

Major intermediaries

Depository Institutions
    Commercial Banks
    Savings Institutions
      (Savings & Loan Associations, Mutual Savings Banks)

Contractual Institutions
    Life Insurance Companies
    Property and Casualty Insurance Companies
    Pension Plans

Investment Companies
    Mutual Funds
    Money Market Funds
    Real Estate Investment Trusts

Private Investment Companies
Finance Companies
Investment Banks

EXERCISE 1 ➤
Saver or capital user?

Saver or Capital User?

Who acts as the saver? the capital user?

Example

saver	You make an annual life insurance payment

1.		You make an extra payment into your pension fund.
2.		You borrow $150,000 to buy a flat.
3.		Your teenage cousin, Biff, has a construction job in the summer and miraculously doesn't spend every cent he earns.
4.		Uncle Rollo buys a vintage Harley Davidson motorcycle using his VISA card.

INTERMEDIARIES' ACTIVITIES AND PRODUCTS

Debt and Equity

> The big question: If I invest money, what's my risk of losing it?

One of the big questions savers have in the capital markets is: if I make an investment, what is my risk of losing my money?

The capital markets organize their products or "instruments" into categories according to the products' risk. The best way of thinking about this is to imagine a spectrum with high-risk products on one end and low-risk products on the other. These products allow the savers, intermediaries and capital users to get together. Large capital users issue securities in the forms of loan agreements, bonds, notes, mortgage loans, commercial paper, common stocks etc.

These securities fall into two main categories: products with contractual claims (debt) and those with ownership (equity).

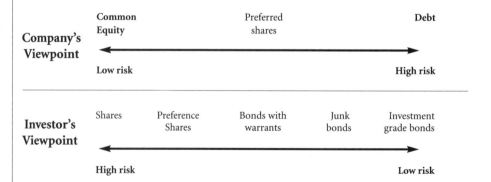

Pure debt

Here the investor lends money out for a certain time and for a fixed payment (usually called **interest** or a **coupon**). The investor can legally demand repayment at the end of the investment period or sometimes sooner if the interest is not paid. A good example of a contractual claim is a bond, which is the most common way governments and large corporations borrow money. In return for receiving funds the issuer gives the investor a piece of paper called a bond. A bond is a legal agreement by the issuer to repay the investor and make interest payments. Normally the issuer promises to pay interest payments periodically and the principal amount at the end of the agreement in one payment. A bond with the capital repayment (called the **principal**) at the end of its life is nicknamed a "bullet" bond.

> KA-PWEEEE!
> Bullet bonds!

Pure equity

> Invest in equity: get a stake in the profits, but no repayment or interest

Unlike debt, equity does not have a repayment period or interest. The investor provides money and does not expect to be paid back. However, the investor expects that some of the profits will be paid to the shareholders in the form of dividends and that his or her stake will increase in value. The investor can get out of the investment by selling it to another investor—through the capital markets. Although an equity investment is riskier than a debt investment it offers the investor a chance to make out big if profits are very high.

The risk spectrum of debt and equity is only relevant for one particular investment opportunity. You can't say that investing in a small Colombian company using a debt product is safer than investing in Coca-Cola's equity. However, making the distinction between debt and equity is important to understanding how the capital markets are organized.

Other products and derivatives

The descriptions above are a simplified picture. Many products in the capital markets department store are in between debt and equity. They help to fulfill the niche needs of particular investors and users of capital.

Barefoot pilgrim

An Aunt Millie who's lost everything in securities trading

EXERCISE 2 ➤
Debt or Equity?

	Debt or Equity?
1.	Which is more risky to hold as an investor: debt or equity?
2.	A company which funds itself with lots of debt has a conservative or aggressive financing structure?
3.	As an investor will you expect a higher return from your equity holdings or your debt holdings?
4.	Which product's return is dependent upon a company's profitability; debt or equity?
5.	Is a company obliged to make interest payments to its debt investors?

THE CAPITAL MARKETS DEPARTMENT STORE

Now let's take a closer look at the products available in the capital markets department store. We'll start with various kinds of debt and move through the risk spectrum to equity.

Loan department

The loan department is split into two divisions: retail and commercial. Let's start with retail. The retail division is full of customers like you or me: we want loans to buy houses (mortgages) or cars or to take the holiday of a lifetime. Some of them are sitting down with bankers like Citibank or Bank of America in the US or Barclays and Lloyds in the UK. Others are filling out applications for credit cards. Credit cards are just loans by another name and delivery system. Still others are talking to their credit unions or finance companies.

The commercial division is full of business people in suits, some representing companies and some representing commercial banks such as Fleet Boston and Deutsche Bank. Their activities are similar to the retail division's, except their numbers are much bigger and involve companies. The companies are signing a variety of different loan agreements split into two broad categories: senior debt loans, and subordinated debt loans.

Senior debt loans

Commercial loans: Senior debt is the least risky **for the bank**

Here the companies are agreeing to take out loans, which will be the first to be repaid if the company goes bankrupt. The interest rate on senior debt loans is among the lowest of all the products being offered in the loan department, but from the bank's viewpoint senior debt is the safest type of loan.

Subordinated debt loans

These agreements are very similar to the senior debt loans, except subordinated loans will be second in line to be repaid in a bankruptcy situation and they have a higher interest rate than senior debt loans. The subordinated debt market is much smaller than the senior debt market.

High yield loans

The riskiest loans!

In one corner where higher risk borrowers congregate the activity is more intense. Bankers are discussing "Leveraged Buy-outs" and companies are saying they want to use loans to purchase other companies. The loan agreements between the banks and companies are very detailed and the interest rates on the loans are significantly higher than most senior and subordinated loans.

EXERCISE 3 ➤
Show Me the Money!

Show Me the Money!

1. ☐   Which type of loan is most expensive for corporations to take out with a commercial bank?

2. In the event of a company going bankrupt and its assets being sold off which loans

   ☐   Will be repaid first

   ☐   Will be repaid last

3. ☐   Which is the cheapest type of loan a company can get from a commercial bank?

THE BOND DEPARTMENT

One floor up the atmosphere in the department store is frenetic. On one side of the floor investment bankers from firms like Goldman Sachs, Merrill Lynch, Morgan Stanley, UBS Warburg and JP Morgan Chase are busy having meetings with Chief Financial Officers and Treasurers of some of the largest companies in the economy. Many of the companies, like Coca-Cola, British Airways, Ford and IBM are household names. You might even find some representatives from governments talking to the investment bankers.

> Where governments shop for money

Bond issues

Instead of talking about loans, the companies and governments are discussing bond issues. The bond issues they are talking about are like loans which are divided into very small pieces, with denominations usually starting at $1,000. A bond issue is the sale of thousands, sometimes millions, of these bonds. An important benefit of the bond is that the purchaser (the saver or investor) can easily re-sell the bonds to other investors. Therefore bondholders are prepared to accept a lower interest rate than commercial banks would charge for their loans.

> Bonds: easy to sell because they're in small units

As with bank loans, some bonds have greater credit risk than others. The ones which are the safest are called investment grade and the ones with greater risk are referred to as high yield, or occasionally as junk bonds.

Very, very, very short-term bonds: commercial paper

In one corner some bankers and CFO's are discussing a **commercial paper** program. Instead of using commercial bank loans, many very large companies have a program of issuing extremely short-term bonds with lives of less than 270 days. These bonds are called commercial paper or CP for short in the financial markets.

> Jargon for experts: CP means commercial paper

The den of lions

The other side of the floor resembles a high-tech children's playground. The floor is covered with computers with screens full of numbers. Lots of traders or salespeople are working intently. Some are talking in small groups; some are shouting loudly at

> The trading floor: the arena of the capital markets

one another—not always in a nice way. The salespeople are on the telephone, mostly to investors like pension funds and fund managers. On one wall an elongated screen has three-letter codes and numbers rolling horizontally across it and a sign which says "trading floor."

Capital markets and the trading floor

The investment bankers who negotiate the amount and terms of bond issues with large companies maintain frequent contact with the traders and salespeople on the trading floor. The salespeople on the trading floor sell the bond issues to investors. Later on, if the investors want to resell the bond, they can come back to the salesperson, who will resell it to another investor.

Divisions of the trading floor

Gunslinger

A speculative fund manager who buys high-risk stocks

Different parts of the trading floor, called **desks,** specialize in different products. The emerging markets desk sells and trades bonds issued by companies and governments from emerging economies. The high yield desk specializes in bonds whose risk profile and expected return is higher than normal. The investment grade desk trades the largest volume of bonds. The syndicate desk is responsible for managing the process of bond issuance. They regularly monitor market conditions so they can advise potential borrowers on interest rates and the availability of financing.

EXERCISE 4 ➤
Bonds

Bonds	
1. _____	Which are riskier, high yield or investment grade bonds?
2. _____	What type of companies use the bond markets?
3. _____	What benefit do companies get by issuing bonds rather than taking out bank loans?
4. _____	Who are the clients of salespeople?
5. _____	What denominations are bonds issued in?

EQUITY CAPITAL MARKETS

Jargon for experts: making a market and IPO's

On the same side of the floor as the debt capital markets is a section called **equity capital markets.** The equity capital markets are similar in structure to the debt capital markets. Investment bankers talk to large companies about raising money. Instead of bonds, the bankers and companies are talking about issuing shares. Equity salespeople sell them to investors and equity traders buy and sell the stock, **"making a market."** A company's first share issue is called an **initial public offering (IPO).** A second sale of shares is called a secondary offering.

What are shares?

Shares simply represent an ownership stake in a company. Investors (mainly pension funds in the capital markets) give companies money in return for an ownership stake in the company. They receive a share certificate as a record of the transaction. The original investors can resell the shares in the equity capital markets.

Size isn't everything

The equity capital markets are not dominated by shares of large companies, unlike bonds in the debt capital markets. Some of the companies making initial public offerings (IPOs) are relatively small.

Reward rather than risk

Fixed income markets = bond markets

The traders and salespeople in the bond markets (more commonly called the fixed income markets) focus on risk and interest rates. The equity markets concentrate on the growth in a company's profits. A key number for the equity markets is the amount of profit a company is producing per share (usually called **earnings per share**).

EXERCISE 5 ➤
The Equity Markets

The Equity Markets

1. [   ] What ratio do equity investors focus on most?

2. [   ] Do large firms dominate the equity capital markets?

3. What records the fact that a company has sold shares?
   [   ]

4. [   ] Do equity capital markets focus on risk or rewards?

5. What is an IPO?
   [   ]

Role of the SEC

Watch out! The SEC is watching you...

The Securities and Exchange Commission (SEC) oversees the issuance and trading of corporate securities in the US. Its role is to ensure that there is full disclosure and fairness for the capital market players and the securities they issue or buy.

2. TIME VALUE OF MONEY

Many of the transactions in the financial world are based on the **time value of money.** Because it's basic to so many aspects of finance and financial math, you need to learn about the time value of money before you do anything else.

WHAT IS THE TIME VALUE OF MONEY?

The time value of money refers to the value of holding money over a period of time. If you're financially savvy, you will want to get a dollar today instead of waiting a year to receive it. Why? Because you could invest the dollar and generate a return. In other words, there is value in holding the dollar over the year. Your next question is: How big is the return I can get?

Learning to understand the time value of money helps you answer questions like these:

- **Which is more valuable, receiving $1,000 today or $1,030 one year from now?**
- **Should you take that lottery pay-out of $75,000 today or should you choose to receive $18,000 a year for 10 years?**
- **How should you invest £5,000—in a bond that pays £10,000 10 years from now or in an annuity that pays out $1,430 per year for seven years?**

Financial people are interested in three aspects of the time value of money:

Future Value	The future worth of money that you invest today
	What will $100 be worth if you deposit it in a savings account at 5 1/2% and leave it there for three years?
Present Value	The current worth of money you will receive in the future
	What amount of money in today's terms is equivalent to receiving $2,000 a month for five years?
Interest Rates	The average annual return on your money over the life of an investment
	What is the average annual return on my money if I originally invested $100 and received $150 two years later?

Time value of money calculations can answer these questions and many others.

> Money! It's worth more NOW.

Dead cat bounce

A pitiful stock's small rise after it has hit rock bottom. Not to be taken seriously. "Even a dead cat will bounce if you drop it off a tall building."

EXERCISE 6 ➤
The Pitch

The pitch

How much money will you have in the future?

The Pitch

1. [   ] Is it better to receive a specific amount of money earlier or later?

2. Why is there value to investing money over time?

   [   ]

3. [   ] What is the current value of future payments called in financial math?

4. [   ] As an investor, is it better to have a higher or lower interest rate?

5. Is the following question asking for the present or future value?

   How much would I have to invest at an interest rate of 8% to receive $1,000 each year for the next five years?

   ❑ Present Value   ❑ Future Value

FUTURE VALUE, PRESENT VALUE & INTEREST

Future Value

If you deposit 50,000 rials in a savings account at 4 7/8% interest calculated on a daily basis, what will be its *future value* in three years? In other words, how much money will you receive three years from now?

To answer this question, you must understand what affects future value.

Time: The number of years (or months or days) you save for

Rate: The interest rate applied to the money

The **higher** the interest rate, the **greater** the future value of your money.

The **longer** the money sits in the savings account, the **higher** its future value will become.

> **Future Value**
> Future Value = Present Value * (1+ *interest rate*)$^{\text{number of periods}}$

Present Value

You've just received a big bonus. You want to go on a round-the-world trip that will cost $60,000 three years from now. To meet your goal, how much will you need to set aside now in a savings account that pays 6 1/4% interest?

What affects present value? The same factors affecting future value:

Time: The number of years (or days or months) between the future payment and today

Rate: The interest rate applied to the money. In present value problems the interest rate is sometimes called the **discount rate**.

> **Present Value**
> Present Value = Future Value $\div (1 + \text{interest rate})^{\text{number of periods}}$

Jargon for experts: Sometimes people use "Discount rate" when talking about the interest rate

Discount or interest rate

Another term you need to know to understand the time value of money is the **discount** or the **interest rate.**

Most investments show their return as a percentage, usually called the interest rate, the return, or the yield. People find it easy to use percentages to compare investments. The yield or interest rate is simply the average growth of your money over time. The higher the growth, the faster your wealth will increase.

For example, suppose you start your first job after leaving college. Your new boss says, "You can either have a $35,000 lump sum in one year or take $25,000 now."

In other words, the time value cost of having your money one year early is $10,000. However, knowing your dollar return on its own is meaningless unless you can compare it to something. This is where interest rates come in. We compare most investments by the % return they generate. The return helps us compare the time value of money in different situations. Here it is algebraically:

> **Interest Rate**
>
> Interest Rate = $\dfrac{(\text{Original Investment} + \text{Gain on the Investment})}{\text{Original Investment}}$

So the Time Value of Money rate for the situation above is calculated as:

$$\frac{(\$25,000 + \$10,000)}{\$25,000} - 1 = 40\%$$

The return on your money

Your return for accepting the money later is 40%. Now it's easy to make comparisons with other investment opportunities. You can contrast 40% with the interest rate a bank would give you for depositing your savings. Now you can answer the question; do you think 40% is high or low?

> *High. If you think 40% is a low return please tell me where you are depositing your money!*

Therefore when would you accept the money; at the beginning or the end of the year?

> *Accept the money at the end of the year, because you'll get a 40% return for doing so!*

EXERCISE 7 ➤
The Mandate

The Mandate

The Mandate

Using the equations above try the following problems.

1. James asks you to lend him $400,000 for one year to finance a small film. He will give you 50% of the gross, which you estimate to be $1,000,000. What is the return on your money as:

    an interest rate:

    and in absolute $?

2. Didcut Bank Inc. is offering you a loan with an interest rate of 7% per year. You want to borrow $15,000 for one year to buy a car. How much would the total interest and the principal of the loan be at the end of the year?

    Interest:

    Principal:

    Total (Future Value):

3. You work for Pineville Savings & Loan Inc. A customer walks in and tells you they need $13,000 in one year to pay for their daughter's wedding. You look up the current savings rate; it's 6%. How much does the customer have to deposit now to have $13,000 in one year?

    Deposit required:

4. You have £150,000,000 to invest today and can invest it at 7.13% for the coming year. You need £160,000,000 at that time. Will you have enough?

    ❑ Yes   ❑ No

5. You want to have $150,000 in one year's time and can invest today at 8.73%. How much do you need to invest today to generate $150,000?

    Money needed:

Hit the phones

Hit the Phones! Summary

1. The value today of money you will receive in the future is called its present value. The value that money you're holding now will have in the future is called its future value. An interest rate is the average return you receive on your money.

2. The sooner you receive money the better. £100 today is more valuable than £100 in one year's time.

3. COMPOUND INTEREST

> Increase your wealth with interest on interest

So far we have only looked at periods of one full year. There are many situations where people want to save or invest for longer than one year. You must also consider the additional interest that can be earned on the interest your savings or investments give you.

At present we are dealing with small numbers. When you work in the financial industry, you will deal with many millions or even billions of dollars, pounds, yen or euros. Interest on interest can make a big difference.

EXAMPLE

A good example of compound interest is a savings account:

Assume you put $1,000 in a savings account for three years and the interest rate stays unchanged at 10% each year, then:

At the end of the first year you will have:
$1,000 * (1 + 0.1) = $1,100

At the end of the second year you will have:
$1,100 * (1 + 0.1) = $1,210

At the end of the third year you will have:
$1,210 * (1 + 0.1) = $1,331

We can simplify these calculations to one simple equation:

$$\text{Future Value} = \text{Present Value} * (1 + i)^n$$

Where:
i = interest rate per period (also known as the yield)
n = number of periods

So to prove it to you:
$1,000 * (1 + 0.1)^3 = $1,331
In the above example $1,000 is the **principal** and $331 is the **interest.**

We have just combined three equations into one!

> The power of algebra

The formula we just worked out (see the algebra appendix for a full breakdown) is usually known as the compound interest formula.

Compound Interest

$$FV = PV * (1 + i)^n$$

FV = future value
PV = present value
i = interest rate per period
n = number of periods

You can solve three basic problems using this formula:

1. Find a future value

2. Find a Present Value

3. Find an interest rate (or "yield")

Before you run straight for the calculator, beware! Understanding the algebra is absolutely critical to success in financial math. Solve the problem using algebra first and then use the calculator.

Warning

EXERCISE 8 ➤
The Pitch

The pitch

The Pitch

1. Find a future value: "How much will I have when I retire?"

    Problem: You invest €50,000 today at 8.12% for 20 years. How much will you have at the end? How much money would you have if you could invest at 8.25%?

    At 8.12% [   ]   At 8.25% [   ]

2. Find a present value "How much do I need to invest today?"

    Problem: You figure that you need €1,000,000 in 20 years. Interest rates are 8.12% per year. How much must you invest today? If interest rates rose to 8.25% how much would you have to invest today?

    At 8.12% [   ]   At 8.25% [   ]

3. How much will a four year university education cost in eighteen years? It costs $120,000 today and the inflation rate is estimated to be 5.0%.

    [   ]

4. If you can invest at an interest rate of 6.50% after tax for eighteen years, how much do you need to invest today in order to have $288,794?

    [   ]

5. You calculate you need €10,000,000 in order to retire in forty years. How much do you need to invest today if you can earn 4.50%?

    [   ]

Warning

Using the calculator

The TVM keys assume that all problems involve either investments (where the present value is negative), or loans (where the present value is positive and the future value is negative). You must make either the future value or the present value negative. Otherwise, when you're calculating an interest rate, you will get a "Error 5" message! Watch this. It's easy to make mistakes.

Notice all the answers including calculator keys have **f** clear **REG** at the top. Making sure all your storage registers are cleared is very important. It's easy to get wrong answers by not starting from a clean slate. Get into the habit now!

INTEREST RATES AND YIELDS

Onion skins

Before there were calculators, bond market people carried around small onionskin paper books of present value tables. They were called "yield books" (thus the famous text, *Inside the Yield Book,* by Sidney Homer).

To find a bond price or yield, you looked up the years and the yield to calculate the price, or looked up the years and the price to estimate the yield. Present value analysis required you to use a "present value table" and a slide rule to calculate prices. Calculating yields took about half an hour to do if the cash flows were not regular like a bond. Complicated analysis required you to use a logarithm table and could take longer. You're lucky you can do this kind of calculation quickly using your calculator!

Yield

$$i = \left[\frac{FV}{PV}\right]^{\frac{1}{n}} - 1$$

FV = future value
PV = present value
i = interest rate per period
n = number of periods

> How much should I save to buy that car next year?

EXAMPLE

You have £50,000 today and want £200,000 in 20 years. At what interest rate (also known as the yield) should I invest? If I wanted £250,000, then how large a yield do I need?

The generic formula for calculating an investment's yield is a cousin of the present value and future value equations:

Putting the problem's numbers in the equation:

$$i = \left[\frac{200,000}{50,000}\right]^{\frac{1}{20}} - 1 = 0.07177 \qquad i = \left[\frac{250,000}{50,000}\right]^{\frac{1}{20}} - 1 = 0.08380$$

Sleeping Beauty

A company which is an undiscovered but attractive takeover target

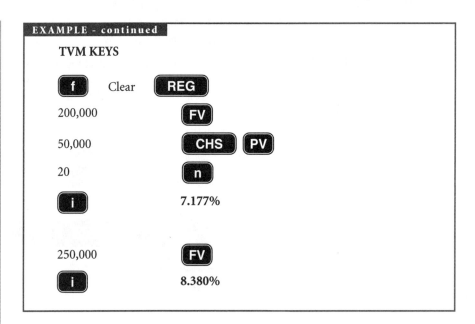

Now try some more questions. This time you will have to decide whether each is a present value, future value or an interest rate problem.

EXERCISE 9 ➤
The Mandate

The Mandate

The Mandate

Write out the equation first, *before* you reach for the calculator! Remember to Clear Registers before each problem.

1. ☐ Find the future value of ¥1,000,000,000 at 6.04% after 10 years.

2. ☐ Find the present value of CHF150,000,000 in 7 years at 5.85%.

3. ☐ Find the yield (interest rate) on an investment that requires €200,000,000 today and promises €1,000,000,000 in 10 years.

4. ☐ What is the future value of €50,000 in eight years at 15.00%?

5. ☐ What is the present value of ¥1,000,000 to be received in three years at 5.45%?

6. ☐ What is the yield on an investment that costs €1,000,000 today and pays €2,500,000 in ten years?

7. ☐ What is the future value of CDN5,000,000 invested at 8.20% for five years?

Hit the phones

Hit the Phones! Summary

1. Compound interest helps you keep track of interest on interest. In other words you can reinvest any interest you receive before the end of the investment period to generate a higher return.

2. Compound interest calculations use the following formula:

$$FV = PV * (1 + i)^n$$

3. The generic formula for calculating the yield of a simple investment with only two cash flows is:

$$i = \left[\frac{FV}{PV}\right]^{\frac{1}{n}} - 1$$

4. Calculating the yield of investments with more than two cash flows is difficult. Don't try it unless you have a calculator.

4. ZERO COUPON BONDS

> Principal, face value or par value?

First a word about regular bonds

If you want to borrow money, typically you go to a bank and take out a loan. Companies can also do this, or they can ask investors to lend them money in return for an IOU ("I Owe You"). The IOU is referred to as a **bond** in the financial markets. A bond is a contract in which the borrower agrees to make specified payments to the lender. Most bonds have regular interest payments called **coupons.** The large repayment made at the end of most bonds is called the **principal, face value** or **par value.**

The benefit of bonds to investors is that they can easily be sold to other investors and that they give the investor a better return than depositing money in a bank. The benefit to the issuing company is that the company has a long-term source of money, often at a lower cost than a bank loan.

ZERO COUPON BONDS

Corporations and governments can raise money by selling bonds with the promise to make one repayment that includes everything: the money borrowed and all the interest. This kind of arrangement is called a "zero coupon bond," which is a bond in which there are no interim payments. At the end of the bond's life, the original money borrowed and the accumulated interest are paid to the investor who owns the bond.

> Cash flow diagrams explain everything

Look at the following diagram of a zero coupon bond. The arrows represent cash flows. Up arrows show cash inflows. Down arrows show cash outflows.

Money paid back = the **par value** or **face value** or **future value**

Time

Money borrowed = price or **present value**

> Once you know how to read them
> ↑ = cash inflows
> ↓ = cash outflows

Zero coupon bond

Hint

The diagram above is called a **cash flow diagram.** Using these diagrams helps you visualize what is going on. It's a great way to catch mistakes early on. Get into the habit of drawing a diagram every time you do a bond calculation.

For every zero coupon bond we can calculate an interest rate which will make the present value equal to the future value over the bond's life. This is called the relevant interest rate, or more commonly, the **yield.**

Wallpaper

Securities which have gone bankrupt or are worthless, good for nothing but papering the walls.

EXAMPLE

A large US electricity generating company, ZapCo, announced its plans to build another five power plants over the next seven years. The CEO, Eileen Lectric, explains to you that she wants $200 million of seven-year financing for the power plants. During the next seven years, the new plants will generate no cash. The company plans to refinance the $200 million bond at the end of the seven years.

You suggest to Eileen that the company should issue a zero coupon bond with a maturity of seven years. You ask the syndicate desk what the yields of seven year zero coupon bonds for ZapCo would be. They tell you approximately 7 7/8%.

Your bond diagram looks like this:

$200 million

7 years

?

We now have a future value problem.
We need to calculate how much the utility company must repay at the end of the seven years. The repayment will consist of both interest and principal.

$$\text{Future Value} = \text{Present Value} * (1 + 0.07875)^7$$

$$340.00 = 200 * (1 + 0.07875)^7$$

When you make your pitch to Eileen Lectric, you tell her she will need to refinance $340 million at the end of seven years.

EXERCISE 10 ➤
The Pitch

The pitch

The Pitch

1. ☐ I just bought a zero-coupon bond with a 10-year maturity and a yield of 6.50%. I paid $5,327.26 for it. What value will it have at maturity?

2. ☐ I want to have $50,000 in 13 years. Interest rates (yields) on 13 year zero coupon bonds are 6.28%. What price will I have to pay for a zero coupon bond that gives me $50,000 in 13 years? This is a present value problem.

3. ☐ What is the price of a five-year ¥100m face value zero coupon bond at 3.02%?

4. ☐ You invest $10,000 today in a 17-year zero coupon bond with a yield of 7.25%. How much will you have in 17 years?

5. ☐ What is the price of a three-year ¥10 million par value zero coupon bond when yields are 2.90%?

> You have to wait until maturity for your interest payment

Zero-coupon bonds don't have interest payments

As you've probably noticed, a zero coupon bond makes no interest payments during its life. The buyer of a zero coupon bond earns a return by the gradual appreciation of the security. You have to sell the bond or wait until it **matures** (comes to the end of its life) to get your cash return. When a zero coupon bond matures both the principal and accrued interest are paid back in one lump sum. Purchasers (investors) of zero coupon bonds frequently use them to plan for a specific investment goal. Knowing their child will enter college in twelve years parents can buy a zero that matures in 12 years.

EXERCISE 11 ➤
The Mandate

The Mandate

The Mandate

1. I see in The Financial Times that 15-year zero coupon bonds are selling at 32 (i.e. 32% of the money the investor will receive at the end of the bond's life).

   ☐ What are the bonds' relevant interest rates (their yields)?

2. ☐ You buy a 10-year, $1,000 par value zero coupon bond for $465. What is your yield?

The Mandate - continued

Some harder questions

3. You buy a 30-year zero coupon bond with a par value of $1,000 at a yield of 8.75% and sell it two years later when 28-year yields are 9.10%. What is your return per year for the two years you owned the bond? This is a three-step question.

| | First, calculate the purchase price. |

| | Next calculate the sale value. |

| | Then calculate the return generated by the investment over the two years you owned it. |

4. You buy a 20-year $100 par value zero coupon bond at a yield of 8.10% and plan to hold it for five years. Your goal is to have a return on your investment of 10% per annum (compounded).

| | What price did you pay for the bond originally? |

| | At what price must you sell the bond? |

| | What yield would that be? |

5. You buy a 5-year zero coupon bond for a price of 63% of par and sell it 2 years later at 83% of its par value. Assume the bond has a par value of $100.

| | What was your yield over the time you held the bond? |

Hit the phones

Hit the Phones! Summary

1. **Bonds are like IOUs.** Bonds record the agreed-upon payments on a loan between an investor and a borrower. The original investor can sell the bond to another investor before the loan agreement ends.

2. **Coupons** are cash payments of interest paid to bond investors.

3. **Zero coupon bonds,** like the name suggests, don't make coupon payments. They have only two cash flows, the initial payment to the borrower and the repayment of the principal and interest to the investor.

4. **Cash flow diagrams** help you avoid mistakes.

5. The buyer of a zero coupon bond receives a return by the **gradual appreciation** of the value of the security.

5. CAPITAL MARKET PLAYERS

So far you've had a general introduction to the major players in the capital markets and the basics of the debt and equity capital markets. Now you'll look at the individual players and their impact on the capital markets in more detail. First let's cover a couple of regulatory issues.

Institutions that must be obeyed

They who must be obeyed!

The **Federal Reserve** or "The Fed" is the central bank of the United States. It keeps a close eye on the commercial banks and savings institutions in the capital markets. The **Comptroller of the Currency** is a separate agency which also oversees national banks. They keep track of how easily individual banks can repay their deposit holders. In addition they instruct commercial banks and savings institutions to keep a proportion of their assets in very liquid (easily sold) low risk securities such as Treasury Bills and cash. These assets are called an institution's liquidity reserve.

COMMERCIAL BANKS

Commercial banks traditionally have been some of the most powerful institutions in the financial system. They raise funds by accepting demand deposits (deposits which can be withdrawn on demand) and savings deposits which are invested for varying fixed lengths of time such as one month, one year etc.

LIBOR floats!

Commercial banks use the money they receive from the deposits to make loans to customers and businesses. Longer-term loans normally have floating interest rates. With a floating interest rate, the rate used to calculate the interest payments is periodically reset based on some well-known index of interest rates such as the **prime rate** or the London Inter bank Offered Rate (LIBOR). **LIBOR** is the interest rate quoted by banks for loans to each other and is a widely used index for establishing interest rates on floating rate loans.

Matching

Most of a commercial bank's liabilities (deposits) are short term. Therefore they are interested in investing these funds they receive in short-term assets. A loan is an asset to a commercial bank, so most of the loans they make are short-term too. The concept of managing the maturities (length) of their assets and liabilities is called asset and liability management. Commercial Banks also try to match currencies and interest rates.

What aspects of matching can a bank consider?

- **Match the currencies**
- **Match the maturities (the length of time until the loan agreement ends)**
- **Match fixed or floating interest rates**

Views on interest rates

Investors are interested in key banks' views

Some banks will intentionally mismatch their assets and liabilities because they have a view or forecast of interest rates and security prices in the future.

F I N A N C I A L   M A T H

Disintermediation

Years ago, major corporations used commercial banks as their major source of loan financing. Presently large corporations bypass the commercial banks and issue bonds. This short-circuiting of the commercial banks is called disintermediation.

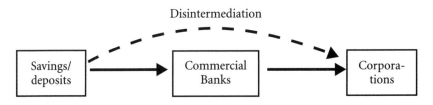

Disintermediation:
a big word for cutting
out the middleman

Glass-Steagall Act

The commercial banks were hit hard when disintermediation began. In addition to reducing their demand for loans, companies reduced their deposits in favor of buying higher-yielding securities in the capital markets. Furthermore, the bonds were issued by the very corporations who used to take out loans from the commercial banks. The Glass-Steagall Act passed in 1933 prohibited commercial banks from underwriting and dealing in corporate securities, so the banks could not help companies issue bonds.

By 2000 the laws were relaxed so that banks could choose to focus on investment banking (issuing securities) or on medium to small business and retail markets. In some cases banks choose both areas.

E X E R C I S E   1 2 ➤
Commercial Banks

Commercial Banks

1. ☐ Do commercial banks have relatively short-term or long-term assets and liabilities?

2. The legislation that prevented commercial banks entering the securities business is called:

3. Describe the concept of matching.

4. Why would a commercial bank **not** match its assets and liabilities?

5. Define the term disintermediation.

Training for Finance

SAVINGS INSTITUTIONS

Just as the commercial banks act as intermediaries for companies and individuals wanting to save or borrow money, the savings institutions (such as savings and loan associations and mutual savings banks) act as intermediaries focusing on individuals.

The maturity of an individual's saving deposits

Before the 1970's, deposits at savings institutions were typically long-term, as individuals put aside money for long-term needs. Historically, the Federal Reserve Regulation Q restricted the return on savings deposits to a maximum of 5.25%. Therefore savings institutions treated these deposits as long-term, fixed-rate liabilities. When the funds were invested in long-term fixed-rate mortgage loans, the asset/liability relationship appeared to be matched.

Savings and loans and the S&L crisis

Interest rates soared during the 1970's and early 1980's. The increase in interest rates (and therefore the cost of funds) contributed substantially to the thrift crisis of the 1980's. The Federal Reserve eliminated Regulation Q. If they had kept it in place, people would have withdrawn their savings in order to earn higher returns elsewhere, such as in money market mutual funds. The crisis is behind us now. Savings institutions are still major lenders for residential mortgage loans, but they manage their asset and liability situations more carefully today.

Credit unions

Credit unions also attract the savings of individuals. Usually credit union members have some affinity such as employment by the same company. The assets of credit unions are concentrated in consumer loans for automobile purchases, home repairs, furniture, etc. In recent years more mortgage loans have begun to appear on their balance sheets.

Deposit insurance

Because it's important to society that individuals' life savings are secure, deposits at banks, savings institutions and credit unions are insured up to $100,000 against loss.

EXERCISE 13 ➤
Savings and Loan

Savings and Loan

1. Are savings deposits considered long-term or short-term liabilities?

   [   ]

2. What was one of the causes of the US savings and loan crisis in the 1980's?

   [   ]

3. What two things make credit unions different from savings and loan institutions?

   [   ]

   [   ]

4. What is the central bank of the United States called?

   [   ]

CONTRACTUAL INSTITUTIONS

Contractual institutions make agreements with individual savers that last over many years. In return for receiving the individual's savings they pay out a lump sum at the end of the contract or tie the payouts to a particular event like death or retirement.

Life insurance

Just insurance, or insurance plus

Life insurance companies are generally involved in selling life, disability and health insurance products to **people.** Life insurance products can be divided into two broad categories:

■ **Products with a savings component (e.g. whole life insurance)**
■ **Products which feature only the benefit of insurance (e.g. individual and group term life insurance).**

Don't let an insurance company go bust!

For those products with savings components, the life insurance companies take in money today and invest it on behalf of the policyholders. In the US, life insurance companies are highly regulated by state governments. As a result of regulation, insurance companies' investment portfolios have to be very conservative. They include government securities, corporate debt (public issues and private place-ments), and commercial mortgage loans.

Insurance companies tend to make long-term and fixed interest rate investments in the same currency as the country in which they insure. These investments match the nature of their liabilities i.e., their promises to pay benefits to policyholders.

You can get annuity contracts from life insurance companies

Life companies also sell pension products. An individual makes payments to the life company during their working years, building up assets that are then drawn down to make payments during their retirement years. These are called annuity **contracts.** Pension products are normally matched with long-term, high quality assets invested in the same country and currency.

Property and casualty insurance companies

Property and casualty companies are generally involved with insuring things: automobiles, homes, and businesses. The individual who owns the car or house makes up-front payments to the insurance company for coverage over a given period. Any claims are made during (and sometimes after) this period. A typical policy generally lasts six months to one year for individuals and several years for business.

How an insurance company makes money from you!

Theoretically the money the insurance company receives in premiums matches the amount of money it pays out in claims and the amount of its expenses. So how does it make any money?

Premiums are paid up-front while claims and expenses are paid over the insured period, resulting in a time lag. Insurance companies can invest money received from premiums in the capital markets before they pay out claims. The return from these investments provides their profits. However, insurance companies can get the model wrong, with disastrous results—witness the Lloyds of London debacle.

> Lives or things? There are insurance companies for each

> Lloyds of London, the world's largest insurance market, almost went bankrupt in the '80's because of very high claims

EXERCISE 14 ➤
Insure It!

Insure It!

1. Do life insurance companies invest in risky or safe investments?
   ❑ Risky ❑ Safe

2. How do insurance companies make money?

3. What is an annuity contract?

4. What are the broad categories of life insurance?

5. Are insurance companies highly or lightly regulated?
   ❑ Highly ❑ Lightly

The *big Kahuna* is a guy who makes things happen. It's a Hawaiian term.

PENSION FUNDS

Pension funds are the *big Kahuna* of the investment world. Pension funds' assets are roughly equal in size to the commercial banks, but are growing more rapidly. Pension funds can be categorized in two different ways.

- **First, they are sponsored by either the government (state and local governments), or private (corporate and union) entities.**
- **Second, their underlying agreement with the covered employee is either with a defined benefit or a defined contribution plan.**

Defined benefit plans

Defined benefit plans promise the employee a formula benefit usually based on length of service. For example, a plan might have the benefit:

> **EXAMPLE**
>
> Employees who worked thirty years and retired at age 65 with average pay at ages 61–65 of $60,000 would have the following annual retirement benefit:
>
> 30 * 2.0% * $60,000 = $36,000
>
> for as long as they lived.

These plans are popular in situations where the work force is unsophisticated and the employee wants a plan he or she can easily understand. Also, if the work force has a high turnover, these plans will be less expensive to the employer.

Defined contribution plans

The defined contribution plan has no specific formula for the retirement benefit a person will receive. Instead the employer agrees to contribute a defined amount that is periodically added to the individual employee's specific investment fund. The fund may be invested in many different investment vehicles, and the risks of these investment results are borne by the employee. A 401-K plan is a popular example.

With a defined contribution plan, the employee gets to choose

The plan might say that the employer will contribute 10% of the employee's salary to a retirement fund each year. The employee can invest the contribution in any of, say, ten different investments (e.g. large company common stocks, intermediate maturity bonds, Pacific Rim equities etc.). The amounts available at the employee's retirement will depend greatly on how successful these investments have been.

Equities: heavy or light?

Generally, defined benefit pension plans have heavy investments in equities across the globe. Defined contribution plans tend to have more conservative investments, but still have more equity focus than commercial banks, savings institutions or insurance companies.

Investment holdings of pension plans

Government and private pension plans have over 50% of their investments in equities. Roughly a third will be in different types of bonds (including high-yield or "junk" bonds). The remainder will be in short-term securities and other assets, such as real estate.

> Does your pension contain junk?

EXERCISE 15 ➤
The Big Kahuna

> What do you think YOUR retirement payout will be?

The Big Kahuna!

1. What two types of retirement plans are there?

2. Which type of security makes up at least 50% of a typical pension fund's assets?

3. Which type of pension plan typically has more conservative investments?

4. What are the two types of sponsors for pension funds?

5. You plan to retire at 60 and your average salary in the five years prior to this was $120,000. Your defined benefit pension plan will pay out 2% of your average ending salary multiplied by the 35 years you worked. What will your annual pension be?

INVESTMENT COMPANIES

Examples of investment companies include mutual funds, real estate investment trusts (REITs) and private investment companies. Investment companies specialize in a particular type of investment asset. For example, a fund may specialize in "small Asian technology companies," or "the stock index," or "medium term investment grade bonds."

Eat someone's lunch

An aggressive competitor beats his or her rivals

Closed or open-ended funds?

Open-ended
Open-ended mutual funds will redeem your investment at its current market value (called net asset value) and give you cash. These type of funds are relatively liquid, in other words they can be converted into cash easily.

Closed end
Closed end mutual funds and real estate investment trusts (REITs) do not redeem shares. Instead you have to sell your shareholding to someone else in order to convert it into cash. Usually the underlying assets of most closed end funds are also illiquid. Examples include real estate and emerging market stocks.

Private investment partnerships

Private investment partnerships are invitation only, privately managed investment vehicles. Like investment companies they typically focus on niche areas, but will make higher risk, less liquid investments. Examples include hedge funds, venture capitalists, private equity investors and leveraged buyout funds.

FINANCE COMPANIES

Finance companies issue securities in the capital markets to raise money. They use the proceeds to make loans to individuals (consumer loans) and businesses (usually for financing inventories and accounts receivable). Car manufacturers have set up finance company subsidiaries to make car loans to individuals and help automobile dealers finance their stock. A successful example is General Motors Acceptance Corporation (GMAC).

Someone out there will lend you money!

Looking for a car loan?

So the next time you are looking for a car loan you might consider a loan from a commercial bank, a credit union, or a finance company. If you are a higher risk customer, you will probably have better luck with a finance company.

EXERCISE 16 ➤
Finance and Investment

Greasing the
wheels

Finance and Investment Companies

1. You have a spotty credit record. Where would you look for a car loan?

2. Are private investment partnerships specialists or generalists?
    ❑ Specialist   ❑ Generalist

3. What is the difference between a closed-end and open-ended mutual fund?

4. What is a finance company?

5. Are the assets of a Real Estate Investment Trust liquid or illiquid?
    ❑ Liquid   ❑ Illiquid

INVESTMENT BANKS

Investment banks provide the grease that makes the whole system run smoothly. They perform numerous capital market functions and help bring together the investors who want to "save" and issuers who want to "use capital or borrow."

Their more important roles include:

Advising and underwriting

Most companies and institutions require guidance when issuing new securities in the capital markets. Investment bankers help institutions by providing up-to-date pricing information and extensive distribution capabilities. They also help issuers determine their funding needs and identify the best approaches to the markets.

Sales and trading

After an investment bank has helped sell a security issue in the market, it will take on responsibility for making a market where the original buyers can sell their holding and new buyers can purchase the securities. Investment banks also buy and sell securities

Making money

Takeovers, acquisitions, targets

to make profits for themselves, an activity called **proprietary trading.** Investment banks can make a great deal of money trading in the markets. They have huge amounts of information at their fingertips and constantly "feel the pulse of the market." However, investment banks can and do make mistakes, as some high-profile cases have illustrated.

Mergers and acquisitions (M&A)/Advisory

Investment banks play key roles in advising both companies who want to buy other companies (known as acquirers) and companies being taken over (known as targets). They use their market knowledge to advise clients on company valuation, negotiating tactics, the structuring and funding of deals. The M&A department of an investment bank is where the lights burn late into the night as bankers work on high-pressure and time-critical deals.

What are the Benefits of Investment Banks?

Although investment bankers with large securities holdings do act as intermediaries, their main role is trading and investing in the capital markets. What are the benefits of having investment banks? Their constant purchasing and selling of securities help make the markets more liquid (so it is easy for investors to buy and sell) and more efficient (so investors and issuers are matched in the best possible way). Their expertise also makes their advice very valuable to their clients.

EXERCISE 17 ➤
Investment Banks

Investment Banks

1. What are the three main activities of investment banks?

2. What is it called when investment banks trade for themselves in the markets?

3. Who do investment banks bring together in the capital markets?

Hit the phones

Hit the Phones! Summary: Who Invests in What

	Short Term Govt. Bonds	Long Term Govt. Bonds	Mort-gage Loans	Common Stock	Consumer Business Loans	Municipal Bonds
Commercial Banks	✓		✓		✓	
Savings Institutions	✓		✓			
Credit Unions	✓		✓		✓	
Life Insurance	✓	✓	✓			
P&C Insuarance	✓	✓				✓
Pension Funds	✓	✓		✓		
Invest Companies	✓	✓		✓		
Finance Companies					✓	
Households	✓	✓		✓		✓

6. ANNUITIES AND PERPETUITIES

Big uglies

Unpopular stocks, usually in unglamorous industries like steel or chemicals

ANNUITIES

So far you have examined an investment with two cash flows, a negative one at the beginning and a positive one at the end. You're now going to look at various ways to receive many positive payments or cash flows over the life of an investment. The first of these is called an **annuity.**

What is an annuity?

An annuity is a series of equal or regular cash flows spread over a time period. A common example is a fixed interest rate home mortgage loan. You receive the loan amount to buy your house (the present value), and in return you make a series of equal cash payments that are usually monthly. From the bank's perspective, this annuity is an investment. The cash flow diagram would look something like this to the bank:

Mortgage Repayments

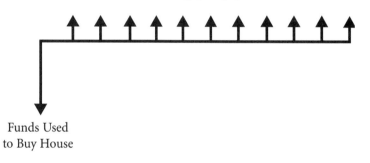

Funds Used
to Buy House

Calculating an annuity's present value

For a given payment amount, interest rate and time period we can calculate the loan provided by the mortgage company using the following equation:

Present value of an Annuity

$$PV = \frac{PMT}{i}\left[1 - \frac{1}{(1+i)^n}\right]$$

PMT	=	Periodic payment
PV	=	present value
i	=	interest rate per period
n	=	number of periods

How much can
you borrow?

EXAMPLE

"I can afford to make mortgage payments of €15,000 per year for 30 years. Interest rates are 7.85%. How much can I borrow?"

$$PV = \frac{15,000}{0.0785} \left[1 - \frac{1}{(1 + 0.0785)^{30}} \right] = 171,284.99$$

TVM KEYS

f	Clear	REG	
15,000		CHS	PMT
7.85		i	
30		n	
PV		171,284.99	

Calculating an annuity's payment

To calculate an annuity's payment, solve for PMT rather than PV:

Work those
formulas!

Payment of an annuity

$$PMT = \frac{PV \cdot i}{\left[1 - \frac{1}{(1 + i)^{n}} \right]}$$

PMT	=	Periodic payment
PV	=	present value
i	=	interest rate per period
n	=	number of periods

EXAMPLE

I want to borrow £200,000 at 8.10% to buy a house. I plan to repay it over 15 years with equal annual payments at the end of each year. What are my annual payments?

$$PMT = \frac{200,000 \cdot 0.0810}{\left[1 - \frac{1}{(1 + 0.0810)^{15}} \right]} = 23,508.77$$

TVM KEYS

f	Clear	REG
200,000		PV
8.10		i
15		n
PMT		(23,508.77)

Cats and dogs

Speculative stocks with no track record of financial results

Calculating the yield of an annuity

There is no simple way to calculate the yield of an annuity using algebra. Use the calculator instead.

EXAMPLE

What is the rate on my loan? I borrowed $100,000 and I make a payment of $14,231.17 each year for 10 years.

TVM KEYS

f	Clear	REG
100,000	PV	
14,231.17	CHS	PMT
10	n	
i	**6.990%**	

Calculating the future value of an annuity

We can calculate the future value of an annuity by rearranging the equation:

Future value of an annuity

$$FV = \frac{PMT}{i}\left[(1 + i)^n - 1\right]$$

FV = future value
PMT = Periodic payment
i = interest rate per period
n = number of periods

EXAMPLE

"How much will I have if I save €20,000 each year (at year end) for 20 years and invest the savings at 9.00%?"

$$FV = \frac{20,000}{0.09}\left[(1 + 0.09)^{20} - 1\right] = 1,023,202.39$$

TVM KEYS

f	Clear	**REG**
20,000	**CHS**	**PMT**
20	**n**	
9	**i**	
FV	1,023,202.39	

EXERCISE 18 ➤
The Pitch

The pitch

The Pitch

1. [ ]   Find the present value of five payments of ¥1,000,000 at year end using an interest rate of 4.03%.

2. [ ]   Find the payment for a mortgage loan of CHF 200,000,000 for seven years at 8.50%.

3. [ ]   Find the future value of an annuity of $12,000 per year (at year end) for ten years at 9.00%.

4. [ ]   Find the yield for an annuity of AUS100,000 per year for nine years that can be purchased for AUS750,000.

PERPETUITIES

A perpetuity is a series of even cash flows or payments that goes on forever, i.e., in perpetuity.

Perpetual motion? No, perpetuities!

Never-Ending Stream of Positive Cash Flows

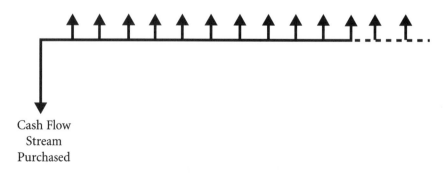

Cash Flow Stream Purchased

The relationship between payment, present value and yield is very simple:

Payment, Present Value and Yield

Payment:

$$PMT = PV \cdot i$$

Present Value:

$$PV = \frac{PMT}{i}$$

Yield:

$$i = \frac{PMT}{PV}$$

PMT	=	Periodic payment
PV	=	present value
i	=	interest rate per period
n	=	number of periods

Never-ending bonds

In 1819 the British government issued bonds called Consols (short for "Consolidated") in order to consolidate its debt from the Napoleonic wars. They are still outstanding. One issue has a payment each year of £4.00. How much is this Consol worth if its appropriate yield is 9.03%?

$$PV = \text{Price} = \frac{£4.00}{0.0903} = £44.30$$

If the Consol is selling for £35.50 what is the yield?

$$\text{Yield} = \frac{£4.00}{£35.50} = 0.11268 = 11.268\%$$

Preferred shares are perpetuities

Another example of a perpetuity is a preferred share. These are shares companies issue with a fixed dividend (payment to the shareholder each year). They usually do not have voting rights and cannot be redeemed.

EXERCISE 19 ➤
The Mandate

The Mandate

The Mandate

1. ▭ What is the price of a preferred stock with a dividend of $6.95 when yields on similar preferred stocks are 8.22%?

2. ▭ Suppose the same preferred is selling for $62.50. What is its yield?

3. ▭ Yields for preferred stocks are 8.15%. Your preferred stock pays a dividend of $6.50 per year. What is its price?

4. ▭ A perpetuity has a price of CHF98,000 and pays an annual payment of CHF10,100. What is its yield?

Hit the phones

Hit the Phones! Summary

1. An annuity is a series of equal or regular cash flows over a particular time period. A good example is a mortgage loan.

2. The equation used to calculate an annuity payment for a mortgage loan is:

$$PMT = \frac{PV \cdot i}{\left[1 - \frac{1}{(1 + i)^n} \right]}$$

The present value of an annuity is calculated using this equation:

$$PV = \frac{PMT}{i} \cdot \left[1 - \frac{1}{(1 + i)^n} \right]$$

The future value of an annuity is calculated using:

$$FV = \frac{PMT}{i} \cdot \left[(1 + i)^n - 1 \right]$$

3. Don't try to calculate the yield of an annuity using algebra. There is no simple way to get the answer. Reach for the calculator instead . . .

4. A perpetuity is a series of even cash flows that go on forever. A good example is preferred stock.

5. Important equations for perpetuities are:

$$PMT = PV \cdot i$$

$$i = \frac{PMT}{PV}$$

$$PV = \frac{PMT}{i}$$

6. Most of the time we calculate annuity values using the calculator's TVM keys rather than the formulas.

7. COUPON BONDS

My name is Bond
. . . *Coupon* Bond

Most bonds in the financial markets are **coupon bonds,** in which an investor buys the bond and then receives a fixed yearly payment called a **coupon** as well as a lump sum when the bond **matures.** This structure is sometimes referred to as a **bullet bond.** The coupon payment is like an interest payment on a loan and is usually expressed as an annual percentage of a bond's face value. For example a bond with an 8% coupon will pay $8 per $100 of the face value. Analytically, a coupon bond is a combination of zero coupon bond and an annuity.

I prefer my
coupons shaken,
not stirred

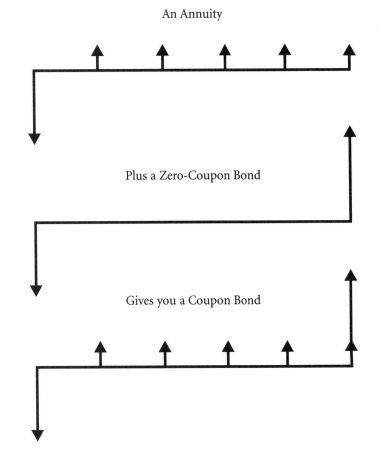

An Annuity

Plus a Zero-Coupon Bond

Gives you a Coupon Bond

Coupon clipping
explained

The origin of coupons

Originally all coupons were detachable pieces of paper with various dates that could be presented to the "paying agent" of the borrower (usually the bank that helped issue the bonds in the first place). They are like a series of post-dated checks for the amount of cash payments due on those dates. The old saying that a person lives by "clipping coupons" means that they clip the bonds' coupons to live on, not that they clip coupons in the newspaper to buy peanut butter.

Warning

Do not confuse a bond's coupon rate with a bond's yield. A coupon is a cash payment that **will not change.** A bond's yield is dependent upon its price and coupon. In the financial markets, coupons are often discussed as percentages of a bond's par value, which can be confusing. If you remember a bond's coupon is the cash payment each year, you should not go wrong.

Cutting coupons is boring

Coupon bonds are pretty cumbersome. Every time a coupon becomes payable you need to take it to the paying agent. Most bonds are now registered bonds. The issuer registers the owners of all the bonds they have sold. Then, when a coupon comes due, they send a check to the person on the register. If you buy the bond, your broker will make sure the register has your name on it.

Diagram, diagram, diagram

Hint

A cash flow diagram is very good way to describe coupon bonds. Cash flow diagrams are used regularly by people working in capital markets. They are an excellent way of avoiding mistakes! The following diagram illustrates the cash flows for a 3-year, 6% coupon bond with a par value of $100 and a price of $95:

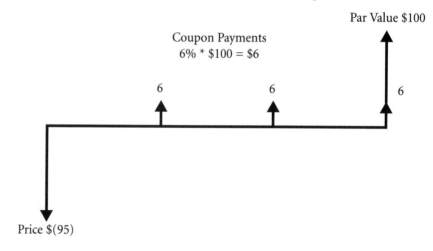

Par Value $100

Coupon Payments
6% * $100 = $6

6   6   6

Price $(95)

% or Actual Numbers?

Bond talk

Bonds can come in many different sizes. Most corporate bonds in the US have a face value of $1,000, municipal bonds $5,000 and Federal Government Bonds a minimum of $1,000. Most people in the financial markets describe the size of a bond issue in terms of its par value, and price bonds as a percentage of their par value. Using percentages makes the numbers easier to deal with and to compare.

A bond issue, for example, can be described as a "$500,000,000 (par value), five year, 9.00% coupon rate, priced at 96."

EXAMPLE

A large European furniture manufacturer wants to issue $320m of 3-year 9% corporate bonds to finance a facility in the US. The bond was priced at 92% of par. Using actual $ numbers your cash flow diagram would look like this:

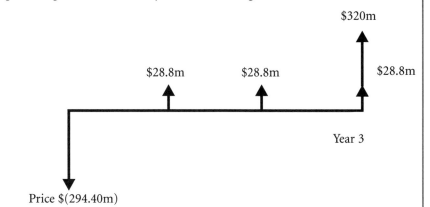

Or you could write out the cash flows like this:

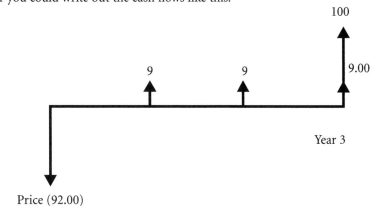

Using percentages is common in finance. It saves time punching numbers into the calculator and helps you avoid making calculation errors.

The pros use percentages

Hint

Par value

Most of the time people use 100% or 100 as a bond's par value. They don't need to know the real par value written on the bond certificate. From now on, if the question doesn't mention a par value, assume it is 100.

Getting yields from coupon bonds

There is no simple algebraic formula for calculating the yield of coupon bonds. Using your calculator is the only easy way to do it.

EXAMPLE

I own a 30-year bullet bond with annual coupons of 7.50%. Yields on similar bonds are 7.92%. Assume the face value of the bond is $100. What could I sell it for? Prices are usually quoted as a percent of par value, so always show the principal payment as 100.

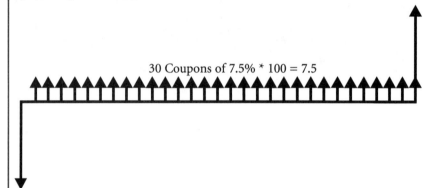

100

30 Coupons of 7.5% * 100 = 7.5

What is the Price using a Yield of 7.92%?

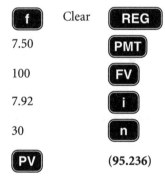

TVM KEYS

f	Clear	**REG**
7.50		**PMT**
100		**FV**
7.92		**i**
30		**n**
PV		**(95.236)**

Now suppose the bond's price is 103.50. What is its yield?

TVM KEYS

f	Clear	**REG**	
7.50		**PMT**	
100		**FV**	
103.50		**CHS**	**PV**
30		**n**	
i		**7.212%**	

Discount or premium?

If a bond's yield is greater than its coupon rate, it will sell at a discount (below face value), and if a bond's yield is less than its coupon rate, it will sell at a premium, or above face value.

Hint

Sanity check

The observation above provides a quick check on calculations. If you calculate a yield for a bond which is selling at a premium that is higher than the bond's coupon, you know you have made a mistake.

EXERCISE 20 ➤
The Pitch

The pitch

The Pitch

Remember to draw the cash flow diagrams!

1. [ ] Find the price of a 10-year 8.75% annual coupon note when 10-year interest rates are 8.10%.

2. [ ] What is the yield on a 7-year note with 6.00% annual coupon and whose price is 97?

3. [ ] Find the price of a 5-year, 6% coupon bond when yields are 6.25%.

4. [ ] Find the price of a 25-year 12% coupon bond when yields are 8.22%.

BACK TO . . . ZERO COUPON BONDS

Remember zero coupon bonds? Now you should be able to understand what a zero coupon bond is—a bond without coupons. If a bond has no coupons, the investor must be enticed to buy the bond by a big discount to its face value.

If five-year zero coupon bonds are trading at yields of 8.00%, what is a fair price for a 5-year, $100 par (face) value bond?

The cash flow diagram looks like this:

100

Year 5

?

This is a simple present value problem. You can solve it using either the calculator or algebra:

$$\text{Present Value} = \frac{\$100}{(1 + 0.08000)^5} = 68.058$$

Notice that calculating the price of zero coupon bonds is much easier than calculating normal bond prices!

EXERCISE 21 ➤
The Mandate

The Mandate

The Mandate

1. [ ]   What is the yield on a 5-year 6% coupon bond when its price is 101?

2. [ ]   A 5-year bond's price is 98 and its yield is 8.40%. What is its coupon?

3. [ ]   What is the yield on a 30-year, 6% coupon bond selling at 110?

4. [ ]   You buy a 10-year 7.50% coupon bond at a price of 92 and hold it for one year. You sell it at the end of the year when yields on 9-year bonds are 7.10%. What was your return?

5. [ ]   You buy a 10-year 8.00% coupon bond at a price of 110 and hold it for one year. At what yield must you sell the bond in order to earn a 10.15% return for the year? **Hint:** remember you receive the coupon at the end of the year.

Hit the phones

Hit the Phones! Summary

1. Coupon bonds are effectively combinations of zero coupon bonds and annuities. The principal part of the bond is repaid at the end of the investment.

2. Don't confuse coupon rates with yields. Coupons are cash flows, not interest rates. Coupons just look like interest rates because they are described as a percent of the final repayment of a bond, also called its par or face value.

3. Drawing the cash flow diagram helps you avoid mistakes.

4. A bond with one repayment of all the principal at maturity is called a bullet bond. Bullet bonds are the most common type of bonds.

5. Most people use the percentages rather than the actual numbers when making bond calculations.

6. There is no simple way of calculating the yield on coupon bonds. Reach for the calculator instead.

7. Sanity check yourself at the end of a calculation. Does it look right?

8. A zero coupon bond is a normal bond without coupons.

Due Diligence: Annuities, Perpetuities & Coupon Bonds

1. [   ] You borrow $100,000 using a mortgage loan. The interest rate is 1% per month and the loan is to be repaid in 120 months. What is your monthly payment?

2. [   ] A British Consol (a perpetual bond) pays £2.50 each year. Interest rates for perpetuities like this are 6.31%. What is the price of the Consol?

3. [   ] You can buy a 7-year bond with a yield of 6.90% and a price of 98. What are the coupon payments?

4. [   ] You plan to save £1,000 each year for the next ten years. Your savings will earn 7.50%. How much will you have at the end?

5. [   ] What is the present value of an annuity that pays £50,000 per year at year end for twenty years when the required interest rate is 9.00%?

Due Diligence ANSWERS

1. 1,434.71

2. 39.62

3. 6.530

4. 14,147.09

5. 456,427.28

8. RECENT DEVELOPMENTS IN THE CAPITAL MARKETS

> To investors, liquidity is a virtue

SECURITIZATION

Investors like liquidity: the ability to sell an investment quickly. If an investment is illiquid, investors will demand a higher return. Apart from an investment being unpopular, large unit prices (like real estate) and tailor-made contractual obligations (such as loan agreements) also make investments illiquid.

Creating liquidity

To create liquidity, bankers take a portfolio of illiquid investments and issue bonds representing an ownership stake in the portfolio. The interest payment on the bonds is linked to the return on the illiquid investments.

EXAMPLE

Pineville Savings and Loan had loaned $300 million worth of mortgages in the last three years. These mortgages are recorded on Pineville's balance sheet as an asset. Pineville was worried about owning such a large amount of illiquid assets. Jim Hodges, an investment banker in New York, suggested to Buddy Collins, Pineville's CEO, that he should securitize the mortgages. Jim sat down with Buddy and explained how it worked:

First, all the mortgage loans are put into a trust created solely for the purposes of the transaction. We'll call the trust Mortgage Co. Initially Pineville owns 100% of the Mortgage Co.

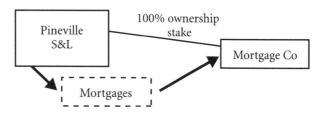

Unfreezing frozen assets

EXAMPLE - continued

Mortgage Co then goes to the financial markets and sells securities representing small stakes in Mortgage Co. The cash generated by these sales is returned to Pineville in return for relinquishing the ownership rights to the mortgages.

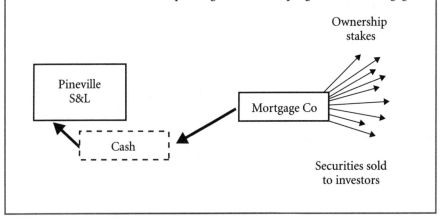

Pineville has now turned $300m worth of mortgages into cash. The process of selling securities linked to an asset portfolio is called **securitization.** The Investors who bought the securities of Mortgage Co (known in the financial markets as **mortgage backed securities**) can easily resell them to other investors. Other common forms of securitization are notes issued against credit card receivables (called "cards"), and notes issued against pools of automobile loans (called "cars").

Securitization generates much more fluid and broader markets for illiquid assets. Consequently, investors are willing to accept a lower return on these assets. Institutions like Pineville use securitization to help reduce their mortgage rates to customers and become more competitive.

GLOBALIZATION

Modern communications and information systems have enabled investors and issuers to look for investing and funding opportunities on a worldwide basis. The capital markets are increasingly global markets. Investors in the Middle East who are looking for investment opportunities can easily access European, North American, and Pacific Rim capital markets. Companies in the US don't just look to American capital markets for funding. They may consider European or even Far Eastern markets.

The process of globalization has triggered consolidation in the financial services industry, particularly among commercial banks, investment banks and insurance companies.

It's a small, small, small, small world these days

> The world has gotten much more complex, with advantages for capital markets players

SPECIALIZATION

The "active players" in the capital markets are increasingly specializing in one particular product area. Specialization has occurred due to several forces.

1. Selling new securities to investors, the **underwriting and distribution process, has become much cheaper and faster.** Smaller, targeted issues of new securities can be made without incurring the large fixed costs historically associated with an underwriting.

2. Mutual funds have grown exponentially. **Funds can now specialize in particular sectors or instruments without becoming uneconomically small.**

3. In the 1960's and 1970's companies tried to diversify their businesses to help reduce fluctuations in profits. In the late 1980's and 1990's companies realized their shareholders were not interested in "smoothed profits." Investors can easily diversify their holdings of stocks so one company's performance alone would have a negligible impact on their portfolio. **Demand increased for stocks representing "pure plays,"** in other words companies which were focused on one business, so investors could easily understand them, and company managements could more easily manage them.

GROWTH OF DERIVATIVES

Derivative securities, which are investments linked to the performance of another asset, have become commonplace in helping meet the financing needs of issuers and the capital needs of investors. Interest rate and currency swaps are two types of derivatives which can help an issuer "swap" from one type of funding to another. For example, a borrower wanting pound sterling financing might consider borrowing funds in Japan in Japanese yen and arranging for a currency swap that converts the yen cash flows into pounds sterling cash flows. The issuer's financing cost is reduced if funding opportunities are much cheaper in Japan. Such packages have greatly opened funding possibilities for issuers and investment possibilities for investors.

EXERCISE 22 ➤
Developments...

Developments in the capital markets

1. ☐ Does securitization lower or increase funding costs?

2. What are "pure plays"?

☐

3. Describe the process of globalization.

☐

4. ☐ What are derivative investments linked to?

5. Name two factors contributing to specialization in the capital markets.

☐   ☐

9. IRREGULAR CASH FLOWS

> Tsk! Tsk!
> Shame on you!

Badly behaved cash flows

Many business problems have cash flows that are not as well behaved as zero coupon bonds, annuities and bullet bonds. Instead, the cash flows vary in size from year to year, sometimes quite dramatically. The concepts of present value, Future Value and interest rate (or yield) apply just as well, but we can't use the time value of money keys on the calculator as they are too inflexible.

Hint

The calculator to the rescue!

The HP-12C Cash Flow keys are there to help you with problems where the cash flows are "badly behaved" or irregular. They are blue on the second row, left center.

Clear the cash flow register by pressing **f** Clear **REG** at the beginning of each problem.

EXAMPLE

Annabel set up a savings plan with Sure Bet Savings. She initially invested $100, then withdrew $50 at the end of the first year and $80 at the end of the second year. Her cash flows looked like this:

Time	Cash Flow
0	($100)
1	50
2	80

What was the yield on Annabel's investment?

Using the Calculator:

Guessing games
pay off in IRR

The internal rate of return: another name for the yield

Finding the yield of an investment with irregular cash flows isn't easy. It is found by trial and error. The calculator makes a series of guesses until it finds the correct answer. As a result, you can't use algebra to solve these problems.

The yield is the interest rate at which the present value of all cash inflows is exactly equal to the present value of all cash outflows. A more common name for the yield of non-bond investments is the **internal rate of return** (or **IRR**).

Net present
value: another
must-know

What's my $ gain on the investment?

Alternatively, Annabel *(example on previous page)* could ask for her net gain on the investment, measured in today's money. Her net gain is the present value of the cash inflows less the present value of the cash outflows, also known as the **net present value** or **NPV** for short. Said another way, it is the present value of all her cash flows including her initial investment.

You can calculate an investment's net present value by adding up all the present values of the cash flows, keeping track of whether they are positive or negative. Remember that first you need an interest rate to calculate the present value of the cash flows:

$$NVP = \sum_{t=0}^{t=2} \frac{CF_t}{(1+i)^t} = -1 + \frac{50}{(1+i)} + \frac{80}{(1+i)^2}$$

Annabel asks you to calculate the net present value of her investment using an interest rate of 10.00%. Using the calculator:

10   **i**

f   **NPV** $11.57

You can also calculate the NPV using algebra:

$$\frac{50}{(1+0.1000)^1} = 45.45$$

$$\frac{80}{(1+0.1000)^2} = 66.12$$

Now calculate the net present value by subtracting the negative cash flows from the positive cash flows:

```
+ 45.45
+ 66.12
- 100.00
   11.57
```

Since the Net present Value depends on the interest rate used in the calculation we will sometimes write NPV(i) to emphasize the point.

Making money

How you would explain the answer to Annabel

The present value of the $50 and $80 cash flows using a 10% interest rate is $111.57. If Annabel invested her money elsewhere at a rate of 10% she would have to deposit $111.57 today to receive these two cash flows in the future. In this case, however, the price is only $100 rather than $111.57, so she makes a "profit" or a gain in present value terms of $11.57.

Another way of looking at the same issue

Another way of looking at the same issue is to think about the 10% interest rate as Annabel's cost of borrowing money. In other words, if she borrowed the $100 at an interest rate of 10% she would make a profit in present value terms of $11.57.

EXERCISE 23 ➤
The Pitch

The pitch

The Pitch

1. Calculate the net present value at 10.00% and the internal rate of return of the following cash flows:

Time	Cash Flow		
0	(100)	NPV =	
1	50	IRR =	
2	60		
3	20		

2. Calculate the net present value at 8.50% and IRR of the following cash flows:

Time	Cash Flow		
0	(15,000)	NPV =	
1	2,000	IRR =	
2	8,000		
3	10,000		
4	10,000		

3. Calculate the net present value at 12.50% and IRR of the following cash flows:

Time	Cash Flow		
0	(1,000,000)	NPV =	
1	(500,000)	IRR =	
2	(300,000)		
3	1,000,000		
4	2,500,000		

The Pitch - continued

These questions are more difficult.

4. Calculate the net present value at 9.30% and the IRR of the following cash flows:

Time	Cash Flow
0	(100)
1	(150)
2	(100)
3	50
4	50
5	50
6	100
7	100
8	100
9	200
10	300

NPV = ☐

IRR = ☐

5. Calculate the terminal value (last cash flow) that makes the NPV at 10.00% equal to 150:

Time	Cash Flow
0	(1,000)
1	600
2	600
3	Terminal value

TV = ☐

Investment opportunity or discount rate?

Same thing, different names

The interest rate used to discount cash flows has different names depending on the situation it is being applied to. It can be called the **investment opportunity rate,** representing the return on your money from the pool of alternative investments, i.e., the investments you ordinarily invest in other than the one you are analyzing.

Alternatively, the interest rate used to discount cash flows can be called the **discount rate,** representing the cost of the money used to make the investment. Match the relevant name with the particular situation.

Fall out of bed

A stock falls out of bed when its price drops suddenly in response to bad news

EXAMPLE

Let's assume Annabel normally invests her money at her local bank. When Annabel is offered Sure Bet's Savings Plan she has two strategies:

   A. Invest in Sure Bet's Savings Plan and reinvest any early cash flows at her bank generating a 10% return.

   B. Invest only in her bank generating a 10% return.

The results for each at the end of two years are shown in the following table. Any cash flows from Sure Bet's Savings Plan will be reinvested at the bank rate of 10.00% until the end of Year 2.

Time	Strategy A: Sure Bet's Savings Plan			Strategy B: Local Bank Only		
	C/F	Int.	Total	C/F	Int.	Total
0	(100)	0	(100)	(100)	0	(100)
1	50	5	55		0	0
2	80	0	80	100	21	121
Net Gain			35			21

Therefore, at the end of the investment period you will be $14 better off if you chose strategy A. The $14 is the **net future value** of strategy A.

To calculate Investment A's net present value, you must calculate the present value of the net future value:

$$\frac{14}{1.10^2} = 11.57$$

A much faster way of calculating the net present value is simply to discount the cash inflows and outflows.

NPV helps you pick the right investment

To reiterate

The net present value calculation helps you compare an investment's return to your investment opportunity rate (the alternative investment rate of 10.00% here) and show any excess value in present value terms.

Another explanation is that Annabel would have to invest 100.00 + 11.57 in her investment pool (the local bank) at 10% to generate the same cash flows as Sure Bet's Savings Plan.

The Mandate

The Mandate

The Mandate

1. Find the net future value at 9.60% of the following cash flows:

Time	Cash Flow
0	(10,000)	NPV =
1	5,000
2	3,000
3	2,000
4	6,000

2. Calculate the change in net present value of the following cash flows when the interest rate goes up from 9.00% to 9.01%:

Time	Cash Flow
0	0	Change in NPV =
1	80
2	80
3	80
4	80
5	1,080

3. Find the net present value of the following six cash flows at an interest rate of 7.25%:

Time	Cash Flow
1	100	NPV =
2	100
3	100
4	100
5	100
6	100

4. Find the net present value at 6.80% of the following cash flows:

Time	Cash Flow
1	(100)	NPV =
2	100
3	300
4	400
5	500

5. Suppose you wanted to purchase the following cash inflows and the appropriate interest rate was 9.30%. What price would you expect to pay? If you could get them for a price of $2,000, what would be your gain in $s?

Time	Cash flow
1	450	Price =
2	650
3	900	Gain =
4	1,000

The Mandate - continued

6. Calculate the NPV at 10% and 12% of the following cash flows. Can you guess the IRR approximately?

Time	Cash flow
0	(930)
1	80
2	80
3	100
4	100
5	1,100

IRR? = _____

Hit the phones

Hit the Phones! Summary

1. Many business problems have badly behaved cash flows. In these situations, use the cash flow keys on your calculator, or, better still, use a spreadsheet program like Excel or Lotus 123.

2. The **Internal Rate of Return (IRR)** is another name for an investment's yield. The IRR is a more common name for the yield of non-bond investments. The IRR is the rate that makes the NPV = 0. Algebraically, NPV (IRR%) = 0.

3. If someone wants to know the absolute $ gain on making an investment, they want to know the investment's **net present value**.

4. You can think of the interest rate used to calculate the NPV as

    either: **the return on alternative investments (called the investment opportunity rate);**

    or: **your cost of capital.**

5. When doing a calculation involving present value, the rate you use is sometimes called the discount rate, and the analysis is called a discounted cash flow analysis or DCF.

10. MODIFIED IRR

The IRR is not always golden

The previous financial decision problems focused on whether to accept or reject an investment. We used the decision rule:

If NPV > 0   **accept, or**
If IRR > i   **accept (where i is the investment opportunity rate)**

The IRR decision rule which says "make the investment if the IRR is higher than the IRR for the alternative investment" is not always correct. In this section you will explore two circumstances where the IRR test will not make the best use of your money. You'll also learn a modification to the IRR calculation that repairs part of the problem.

Mutually exclusive alternatives

If you have to choose between two investments (i.e., rank them), the IRR may not be a satisfactory guide. Here is an exaggerated example that demonstrates this problem. Suppose you have to choose between investing in either New Canaan Secondhand Cars or Clifton Classic Cars. You only have enough money to invest in one of the companies:

Never forget your common sense!

| | | | Time | | | |
Cash flows for:	0	1	2	3	4	IRR
New Canaan	(100)	100	100	100	200	100%
Clifton Classic	(100)	0	0	0	1,568	99%

Both New Canaan and Clifton Classic require the same initial investment of 100 and are both four years long. New Canaan has a higher IRR than Clifton Classic. However, most of us would choose B if offered one of the two. If asked we would probably explain our choice roughly as follows:

"With Clifton Classic, after 4 years I would have $1,568. With New Canaan I would have $500 plus the interest income I could earn on the early cash flows. The interest income would be nice but I could not earn enough to make up the difference with Clifton Classic."

The theme of this reasoning is quite insightful and correct. It also suggests an avenue for adjusting the IRR calculation to reflect this insight.

What if we knew the rate at which we could reinvest the cash flows?

Assume we can reinvest the early cash flows from New Canaan at, say, 10%. Let's calculate the result after four years for New Canaan including the interest earned on these early cash flows. At the end of four years we would have:

Year	Cash Flow		Result at the end of year 4	
1	100×1.10^3	=	133.1	from year 1 cash flow
2	100×1.10^2	=	121.0	from year 2 cash flow
3	100×1.10^1	=	110.0	from year 3 cash flow
4	200	=	<u>200.0</u>	from year 4 cash flow
Total			564.1	

> Get those cash flows moving!

Just move those cash flows around

If we replace New Canaan's original future cash flows with one $564.1 cash flow at the end of year 4, we haven't changed the value of the investment; we have just changed the timing of the cash flows.

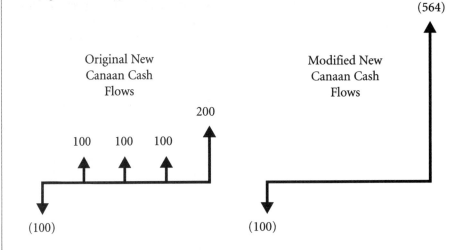

Original New Canaan Cash Flows

Modified New Canaan Cash Flows

> MIRR helps solve some of IRR's problems

CALCULATING THE MODIFIED IRR

After modifying the cash flows we can recalculate the IRR for New Canaan:

TVM KEYS

f	Clear	**REG**
100	**CHS**	**PV**
0	**PMT**	
4	**n**	
564.10	**FV**	
i	**54.113%**	

We call the new IRR of 54.113%, the **Modified Internal Rate of Return** or MIRR. Notice that we made two steps in the calculation above.

Step 1: Find the future value of all cash flows after the initial investment using the reinvestment rate. After step 1 the revised cash flows look like a zero coupon bond.

Step 2: Calculate the IRR of the modified cash flows. There are only two: the initial investment and the future value of the subsequent cash flows.

Modified Internal Rate of Return

The calculation of the MIRR using a HP-12C is a little complicated. It helps to understand how the Cash Flow keys work first.

When you are using the Cash Flow keys, enter the initial cash flow at time 0 by pressing [g] [CF₀]. The calculator resets the number counter, [n], to zero and stores the value of the cash you have input in storage register 0. When you enter the next distinct cash flow by pressing [g] [CFⱼ] the calculator increments n by one and stores the value entered in storage register 1.

When you enter the next distinct cash flow, the 12C increments n again and stores its new value in register 2. Each additional cash flow you enter occupies its own storage register. You can enter up to 20 separate cash flows.

Whenever you wish, you can check the values you have entered by using the [RCL] key to recall the values (RCL 0, RCL 1, RCL 2, etc.).

Press [RCL], then press the number of the register you want to check.

You do not have to check the numbers for the calculations to work, however. You can even edit the cash flows that you have entered by keying in the new value, then pressing [STO] and the number of the storage register you are changing. For example, to change the value of the fifth distinct cash flow to 6,000, input 6000 and press [STO] 5.

Always be sure that you enter [CF₀] at the beginning of the problem and not at the end. The calculator will only process cash flows up through the number in the number counter, n. If you enter [CF₀] last, then you have set n to zero and none of the other cash flows will be processed.

The HP-12C is efficient at calculating net present values, but not so at calculating net future values. The trick is to exploit the calculator's strength when solving MIRR problems. This example may appear complicated at first, but you will quickly find it easy to use.

We are first going to use the Cash Flow keys and then switch to the TVM keys. Here goes!

We want to calculate the MIRR of the following set of cash flows using a reinvestment rate of 8.5%.

Time	Cash Flow
0	(1,000)
1	250
2	300
3	400
4	450

Great feature for doing a sensitivity analysis on the terminal value!

HINT
"A trick"

1. First calculate the present value of the cash flows in periods 1 through 4 as of the end of year 4 using the reinvestment rate of 8.5%. Input the cash flows in the Cash Flow keys as follows

   0 **g** **CF₀** 250 **g** **CFⱼ** 300 **g** **CFⱼ** 400 **g** **CFⱼ** 450 **g** **CFⱼ** .

2. Input the reinvestment rate as 8.5 **i** .

3. Find the NPV of these cash flows by pressing **f** **NPV** = 1,123.12.

4. Change the sign by pressing CHS and enter the value in PV on the TVM keys. Press the following to calculate the NFV as of the end of year 4.

   CHS **PV** 4 **n** 0 **PMT** **FV** = 1,556.49.

5. Finally, input the initial cash flow in PV and press **i** .

   1000 **CHS** **PV** **i** = 11.696%.

The algebraic signs are a little tricky. Remember that in the TVM keys, if you use a negative number in PV, the FV will be positive and vice versa.

EXAMPLE

Calculate the NPVs, IRRs, and MIRRs for the following two sets of cash flows using an interest rate of 9.3%.

Time	Investment A	Investment B
0	(500)	(500)
1	50	350
2	50	200
3	100	100
4	100	50
5	650	50

Answer		
NPV	150.9	131.3
MIRR	15.22%	14.52%
IRR	16.51%	24.43%

Note that the NPV and MIRR give the same ranking; they both tell you that A has a higher value than B. But B's IRR is higher than A's, giving a different result than the NPV and MIRR did. Also note that the profiles of the cash flows are quite different. Investment B favors the IRR with its large early cash flows. So be careful with the IRR when you have mutually exclusive alternatives.

EXERCISE 25 ➤
The Pitch

The Pitch

The Pitch

1. Find the future value in year four using a 9.00% interest rate.

Time	Cash flow
1	100
2	200
3	300
4	400

Value in period four = [   ]

2. Find the future value in year 10 at 8.00%.

Time	Cash flow
1 to 5	70
6 to 9	90
10	1,090

Value in period ten = [   ]

3. Find the future value in year ten of the following coupons at 7.55%.

Time	Cash flow
1–10	80

Value in period ten = [   ]

> A lot of different names for the same useful concept

Different names for the Modified Internal Rate of Return

Many investors worry about reinvestment risk and find the MIRR concept very appealing. It's not surprising that it has been rediscovered many times. Often when people discover the MIRR, they made up a new name: MIRR, Effective Yield, Fully Invested Return, Realized Compound Yield, Holding Period Yield (when applied only for a holding period), Total Return Analysis, etc. Your job is not made any easier with all these names. However, the concept is exactly the same in every case.

> Use MIRR when investment sizes and maturities are the same

When to use MIRR

The MIRR is suitable for ranking investments as long as the **lives** are the same and the **investment size** is the same. The lives can easily be made equal by calculating the MIRR using the longer of the two lives for both investments. If the investment sizes are different, the MIRR is more difficult to use.

The importance of the reinvestment rate

A simple example shows the effect of the reinvestment rate when you have long investment periods. Suppose that you have a 30-year, 8.00% annual coupon bond selling at par. Assume the reinvestment rate over the life of the bond is 8.00%. At maturity, over 90% of the value you have is from the reinvested coupons and less than 10% is from the principal payment. The reinvestment rate is critical in determining the value of the investment:

For a 30-Year, 8.00% annual coupon bond at par

Reinvestment Rate	Proportion of Value from Reinvested Coupons	MIRR
6.00%	86%	6.863%
8.00%	90%	8.000%
10.00%	93%	9.237%

Note that the MIRR depends on the value of the assumed reinvestment rate. We will occasionally use the notation MIRR (i) to emphasize this point.

The MIRR retains its popularity because many people prefer to think of returns as percentages rather than as actual money amounts.

EXERCISE 26 ➤
The Mandate

The Mandate

Hit the phones

The Mandate

1. Calculate the MIRR of the following investment using a reinvestment rate of 10.50%.

Time	Cash flow
0	(1,000)
1	200
2	500
3	600

MIRR = _____

2. Calculate the realized compound yield on RCY for a 5-year, 8% coupon bond selling at 103 using a reinvestment rate of 7.25%:

RCY = _____

3. Calculate the MIRR at 8.50% for the following two sets of cash flows:

Time	Investment A Cash flows	Investment B Cash flows
0	(1,500,000)	(1,500,000)
1	200,000	700,000
2	500,000	500,000
3	700,000	500,000
4	900,000	300,000

MIRR = _____ _____

Hit the Phones! Summary

1. The IRR is not always a good way of helping to decide between investments. Don't use the IRR if the investments you are comparing have very different cash flow profiles, different sizes, or are different maturities.

2. The **Modified Internal Rate of Return (MIRR)** uses a constant interest rate to artificially change the timing of an investment's cash flows.

3. Follow two steps to calculate the MIRR:

   i. Find the future value of the cash flows (except the initial investment) using your chosen reinvestment rate.

   ii. Calculate the IRR of the modified cash flows.

4. The MIRR has many different names, including realized compound yield, effective yield, fully invested return and total return analysis, to name a few.

5. Use the MIRR as long as the investment size is the same.

6. The MIRR is very useful when you have investments with long lives. It helps capture the value of being able to reinvest interim cash flows.

11. MULTIPLE IRRS

Another problem with the IRR!

Most investments only have one change in the sign of the cash flows—a negative initial investment followed by a series of positive cash flows. The cash flows change signs only once over the life of the investment.

EXAMPLE

A **bullet bond** has an up-front payment followed by a number of positive cash flows:

A **new company** start-up may require investment over a number of years before it generates positive cash flows.

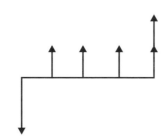
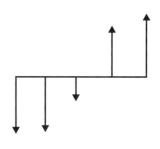

However, some investments have more than one sign change. For example:

Cash flows that change signs more than once

EXAMPLE

A mining company invests in a new mine and generates positive cash flows from producing minerals. When the mine is exhausted the mining company must spend money to decontaminate the site.

An investor buys a Boeing 747 and leases it to an airline. The investor borrows part of the 747's purchase price. At the beginning, the investor makes a down payment for the aircraft. For the next few years, the airline pays lease payments to the investor, who pays principal and interest on her borrowing. There are positive tax benefits at this point. Then the cash flows turn negative as the airline repays the loan used to buy the plane. Finally, there is a positive cash flow from the sale of the plane.

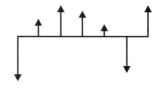

More than one
IRR? How can this be?

Now for some philosophy

The French philosopher and mathematician René Descartes explored the problems of cash flows changing signs and calculating IRRs. He proved **Descartes' Rule of Signs** (paraphrased):

> *"The maximum number of IRRs is equal to the number of sign changes in the cash flows."*

Note the importance of the word *maximum.* There may be fewer IRRs than the maximum number. In the previous examples of the mine and the lease of the 747, there were a maximum of the two IRRs for the mine investment, and a maximum of three IRRs for the lease of the 747.

EXAMPLE

Let's explore an investment with these characteristics:

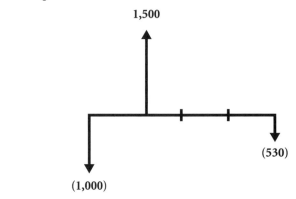

The net present value equation is:

$$NPV(i) = (1,000) + \frac{1,500}{(1+i)^1} + \frac{(530)}{(1+i)^4}$$

Net present value profiles

We can graph the relationship between the interest rate and the net present value for the above investment. The curve illustrates the different net present values for different interest rates.

The NPV profile for the above investment is :

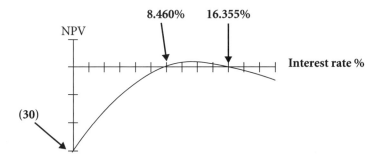

The IRR and net present value

Remember, the IRR is the interest rate where the net present value of an investment is zero. In this case the NPV is zero for two different interest rates as the curve crosses the axis twice. Also notice the NPV is (30) when the discount rate is zero. Get the (30) by simply adding up the cash flows.

Understanding the curve's shape

When the interest rate is very small, the largest impact from discounting is on the last cash flow because of the 4th power in the expression's denominator. Since this term is negative, when it gets smaller, the NPV as a whole rises. Next, as you continue to increase the interest rate further, the final term becomes so small its contribution to the NPV is negligible.

Eventually, a high interest rate starts to have a significant impact on the other positive cash flow. Its reduction in present value causes the whole NPV to fall. The initial cash flow is already a present value and is unaffected by changes in the interest rate.

EXERCISE 27 ➤
The Pitch

The pitch

The Pitch

1. Use the cash flows in the above example and the cash flow keys in your calculator to calculate the net present value for interest rates of: 0%, 3%, 6%, 9%, 12%, 15%, and 18%.

NPV

0%

3%

6%

9%

12%

15%

18%

The Pitch - continued

2. Use the cash flows below and calculate the NPV for values of interest rates of 0%, 3%, 6%, 9%, 12%, 15%, 18%, and 21%. Draw a graph showing NPV on the vertical axis and I% on the horizontal axis. Where would you guess the IRR(s) would be?

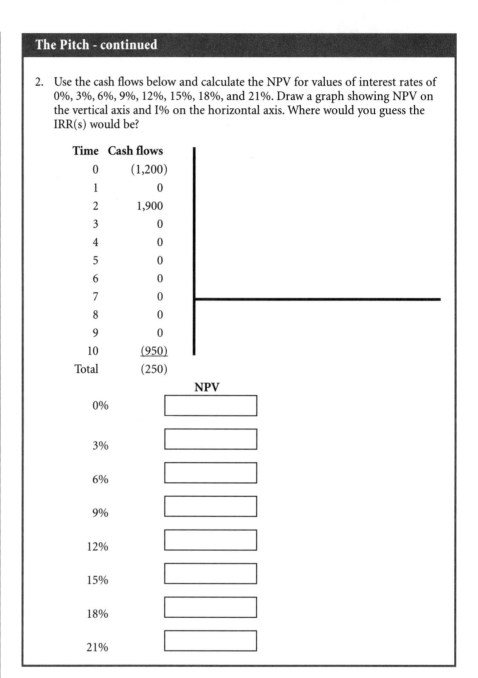

Time	Cash flows
0	(1,200)
1	0
2	1,900
3	0
4	0
5	0
6	0
7	0
8	0
9	0
10	(950)
Total	(250)

NPV

0%

3%

6%

9%

12%

15%

18%

21%

Guessing
games

Two or more sign changes and the HP-12C

If you attempt to calculate the IRR for the above example, the calculator displays the message ERROR 3.

The calculator cannot solve the problem, since there is more than one IRR and thus more than one answer. In this situation you have to give the calculator a reference point to start looking for an IRR. You have to key in a guess of what the IRR could be and then press **CLX** then **RCL** **g** **R/S**.

The ERROR 3 message is first, a warning that a multiple rate problem may exist, and second, an invitation to guess an IRR so as to initiate a search. Here the starting point IRR guess is important, because the IRR you eventually get depends on where you begin searching.

Try it using the above Pitch question 1. Key in 5% as your first guess, then press **RCL** **g** **R/S**. The IRR comes out as 8.460%. If you try 20% the IRR should be 16.355%. These are the two places where the NPV profile crosses the horizontal axis, i.e. where the NPV = 0, and where IRRs are to be found.

Interpreting the results

Now let's try to interpret these results.

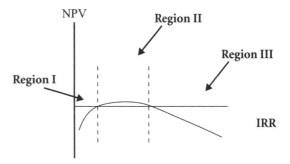

If you are in Region I where your cost of capital or your investment opportunity rate is less than 8.46%, then don't invest in the project because your NPV is negative. If you are in Region II where your cost of capital or reinvestment rate is between 8.460% and 16.355%, you should invest since it has a positive NPV. In Region III, where your cost of capital or investment opportunity rate is over 16.355%, you should not invest as your NPV would be negative.

Here is the interpretation:

- **In Region III we are in a similar situation as with regular investments; where the investment opportunity rate is high, there will be a loss in present value if funds are diverted away from the high earnings of the investment opportunity pool.**

Making money

■ In Region II, the net present value is positive. The investment will increase your net worth.

■ The counter-intuitive situation is in Region I. Here is why you should not invest:

Consider an investor with a low investment opportunity rate, such as a schoolteacher who ordinarily invests in CDs that earn 5%. After the initial investment and the first year he has a profit of $450 after considering the cost of borrowing from his savings account for one year. His profit must be reinvested for the next three years. At 5% it will not grow large enough to make the $530 payment in Year 4. That is why the schoolteacher should not invest in this project.

It is totally wrong to say "I have two IRRs of 8.46% and 16.35%. Both are above my investment opportunity rate, so the investment must be a good one."

Totally wrong!

Warning

Multiple IRRs

Multiple IRRs are reasonably rare. They occur in special investment situations such as the petroleum industry, in the leasing business where investment and financing packages are combined, and where derivative securities are combined in various packages. Whenever one set of cash flows is subtracted from another there is a stronger possibility of multiple sign changes in the result, and therefore possibly multiple IRRs.

EXERCISE 28 ➤
The Mandate

The Mandate

The Mandate

1. Consider these investments

Time	X	Y	Z
0	(1,000)	(1,000)	(1,000)
1	0	500	(100)
2	0	(800)	(100)
3	0	(200)	500
4	0	600	800
5	2,300	2,000	2,000

What is the *maximum* number of IRRs for each?

X = [   ]

Y = [   ]

Z = [   ]

The Mandate - continued

2. You can invest in the following project. What are its IRRs? How would you interpret them? Draw the net present value profile on the graph provided:

Time	Cash flow
0	(500)
1	0
2	900
3	0
4	0
5	0
6	0
7	0
8	0
9	0
10	(600)

NPV

IRR

IRRs =

3. Find the IRR(s) for the following cash flows:

Time	Cash flow
0	(550)
1	2,200
2	0
3	(4,400)
4	0
5	0
6	0
7	0
8	9,000

IRRs =

4. Find the IRR(s) for the following problem:

Time	Cash flow
0	(220)
1	300
2	(300)
3	300

IRRs =

The Mandate - continued

5. Find the IRR(s):

Time	Cash flow
0	(220)
1	0
2	300
3	0
4	(300)
5	0
6	0
7	300

IRRs = [   ]

So is the IRR used much?

The IRR may give poor guidance in ranking investments where there are significant differences in investment size, term, or general profile of cash flows. In situations where the sizes, terms, and profiles are fairly close the IRR is reasonably satisfactory. It is widely used by investment managers, for instance, who use yield to decide on selling one bond and buying another.

Hit the phones

Hit the Phones! Summary

1. The philosopher Descartes proved that the maximum number of IRRs an investment can have is equal to the number of sign changes in the cash flows.

2. A net present value profile is the curve tracing the net present value using different interest rates.

3. The IRR is the interest rate which makes the net present value equal to zero.

4. An ERROR 3 message on your calculator means there may be more than one IRR for the investment. Press [CLX] then give the calculator a guess and then recalculate by pressing [RCL] [g] [R/S].

12. ALL-IN-COST & YIELD-TO-MATURITY

IRR from two different points of view

The viewpoint of borrowers and All-In-Cost

Yield to maturity or **YTM** is the IRR of the cash flows from the **investor's** viewpoint; **All-In-Cost** or **AIC** is the IRR of the **borrower's** cash flows. The difference between the All-In-Cost and the yield to maturity is due to the impact of the fees investment banks charge the issuers, and other costs associated with the creation of securities and their issuance to investors.

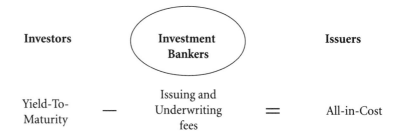

Investors	Investment Bankers	Issuers
Yield-To-Maturity	— Issuing and Underwriting fees	= All-in-Cost

---

EXAMPLE

A borrower is going to issue a one-year 10% annual coupon bond to investors. The 10% coupon rate was selected carefully so investors will pay 100% of the par value to buy the bonds.

From the investors' view the cash flows look like this:

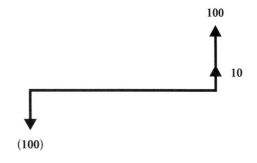

100

10

(100)

And the return or yield to maturity is the IRR of these cash flows or 10%.

EXAMPLE - continued

The borrower's cost of financing

The borrower's view is a bit more complicated in that an investment bank must be paid to find investors. The investment bank earns a fee for performing this service. Suppose that the fee is 1% of the par value. The borrower's cash flows look like this:

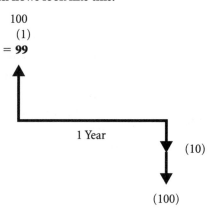

100
(1)
= **99**

1 Year

(10)

(100)

Here the borrower gets 99 and must repay 110 a year later. The IRR of the borrower's cash flows is 11.11%. We call this the All-In-Cost to the borrower.

EXERCISE 29 ➤
The Pitch

The pitch

The Pitch

Remember to draw the diagram when answering the following problems.

1. Calculate the All-In-Cost for the following bond:

   Maturity = 3 years, fee = 1% of par, par value = 100, the coupon of 8% is paid annually and the issue price = 100.

   AIC = _____

2. Calculate the All-In-Cost for a bond with a 7.25% coupon paid annually, an issue price of 99.50, a par value of 100, a 7-year maturity and a 1.5% fee.

   AIC = _____

3. Calculate the All-In-Cost for a 30-year, 6% coupon priced annually, 100 par, priced at 101.5 with a fee of 0.65%.

   AIC = _____

4. You issue a 7-year 8% coupon bond at 101 with a 1% fee. What is your All-In-Cost?

   AIC = _____

The Pitch - continued

Remember to draw the diagram!

5. You issue a 3-year bond at 99.50 with a coupon rate of 6.25%. The issuance fee is 0.65% of par. What is your AIC?

AIC =

FEES

Making money

Underwriting fees

Underwriting fees are very important to investment bankers. If a company wants to issue bonds it will ask an investment bank to underwrite the issue. The investment bank will buy the bonds from the company first before selling them to the investors. Once the investment bank has bought the bonds it will sell them to investors as quickly as it can. The price at which it buys the bonds from the issuer will be slightly lower than the price at which it sells them to investors. The price difference is called the **underwriting spread.** The underwriting spread is usually described as a percentage of the total par value of the issue; say 1 5/8% or 0.65%.

An exception to the rule that underwriting fees are a percent of the par value occurs when the bond is a zero coupon or "low coupon" bond. In these cases, the price is considerably below the par value and the fee percentage is applied to the price.

The underwriting fee rewards the investment bank for taking the risk that it will not be able to sell the bonds to the investors at the issue price.

Issuing expenses

In addition to the underwriting fees paid to the investment banks there are also other issuing expenses. These typically include legal, accounting, printing and other out-of-pocket expenses (including road show drinks!). The company making the bond issue pays for these fees.

Warning

Percent or Actual Numbers?

You already know most people in the bond markets work in percentages when calculating the yields of bonds. It's particularly difficult dealing with fees as some are shown as percentages of the par value and some as absolute $ figures.

> **EXAMPLE**
>
> The Dutch government wants to issue €500m worth of three year bonds with a 5% annual coupon. The investment bank chosen to do the deal, Merrill Barney says it will charge underwriting fees of 1 7/8%. Merrill Barney estimates the issuing costs will be approximately €200,000. The bank plans to sell the bonds to investors at par (100% of their face value).
>
> **You could either work with absolute numbers:**

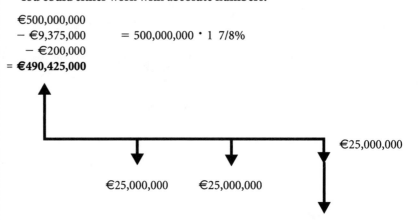

Percentages or absolute numbers?

€500,000,000
− €9,375,000 = 500,000,000 · 1 7/8%
− €200,000
= **€490,425,000**

€25,000,000

€25,000,000   €25,000,000

Or, much more simply, you could diagram **the same problem using percentages** rather than absolute figures and come to the same answer for YTM and AIC:

100
− 1.875   = 200,000 ÷ 500,000,000 · 100
− 0.04
= **98.085**

5

5   5

100

Warning

Beware of making a mistake when calculating the fees as a percentage. It is extremely easy to forget to multiply by 100 when converting a decimal into a percentage.

Calculating the YTM and AIC

Now you can calculate the YTM and AIC for the previous example:

All-in-Cost

Work those keys!

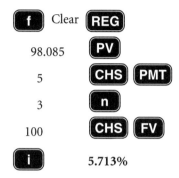

Yield-To-Maturity

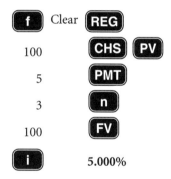

The yield-to-maturity is easier because the investor's cash flows do not involve the investment banking fees and other costs.

EXAMPLE

Here is an example which takes you through the three-step process of calculating the All-In-Cost of a bond:

A borrower issues €500,000,000 (the par value) of 5-year 6.00% annual coupon notes to investors at price of 100.5 (% of the par value). Underwriting fees are 1 5/8% of the par value. Up front, legal, printing, and road show costs are €250,000. What is the All-In-Cost to the issuer?

Step 1: First, calculate the up front costs as a percent of the par value.

$$\frac{250,000}{500,000,000} * 100 = 0.05\%$$

Step 2: Draw a cash flow diagram of the issue in **percentage** terms.

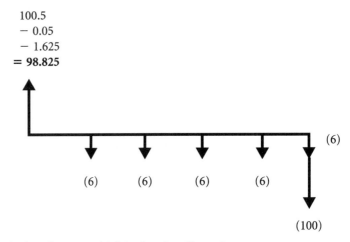

```
100.5
− 0.05
− 1.625
= 98.825
```

Step 3: Calculate the IRR, which is also the All-In-Cost

TVM KEYS

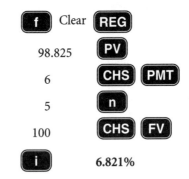

Hint

Checking your results

As you do more and more of these problems you will see how easy it is to make mistakes. You can reduce the likelihood of errors in two ways. First, always, always, always draw the diagram. Second, do a "sanity check" on your answer. Does it look right?

Always check to capture errors. Being just a few decimal places off can spell disaster. Remember, you are dealing with millions, possibly billions of dollars, pounds or euros, so a small error can translate into a significant number.

EXAMPLE

You calculate the internal rate of return of a 3-year bond issued at 95% of par, with a coupon rate of 6%.

If your answer was 5% does it seem right?

No, the coupon is 6% but you also get the benefit of a 5% discount on the purchase so the IRR should be even higher than 6%.

EXERCISE 30 ➤
The Mandate

The Mandate

The Mandate

1. You can buy a 5-year, 6% coupon (paid annually) bond for 98. What is your yield-to-maturity?

    YTM = ▢

2. You can issue a 5-year bond with a £250,000,000 par value at a price of 99.5. Your fee is 0.70% of par and your other up-front costs are £250,000 (printing, legal and road show costs). The coupon rate is 6.25% paid annually. What is your All-In-Cost?

    AIC = ▢

3. You issue €500,000,000 of bonds (par value) with a maturity of 7 years. The fee is 2% of par and the bonds are priced at 100.5. The coupon is 6.75% (paid annually). Other up-front issuance costs are €200,000. What is your All-In-Cost?

    AIC = ▢

4. Calculate the AIC of a GBP 500 million issue with a 15-year maturity, a 7.25% coupon, 2.00% fee, priced at 101.50 with other costs of GBP 200,000.

    AIC = ▢

5. Calculate the AIC of an AUS200 million issue with 6 3/8% coupon rate, 5-year maturity, 1 7/8% fee, AUS150,000 of other issue costs and issued at 100.5.

    AIC = ▢

Hit the phones

Hit the Phones! Summary

1. The All-In-Cost (AIC) is the borrower/issuer's IRR. The Yield-To-Maturity (YTM) is the investor's IRR.

2. For a particular bond issue, the AIC is always higher than the YTM as the former takes into account fees included in the transaction.

3. There are two types of fees in bond transactions:

   i. Underwriting fees described as a percentage of a bond's par value.

   ii. Issuing expenses, given in absolute numbers.

4. When calculating the AIC for a bond issue, be careful to make sure you convert dollars to percentages correctly.

Due Diligence: Irregular Cash Flows, MIRR, Multiple Rates AIC, YTM

1. Find the net present value at 10% and the internal rate of return for the following cash flows:

Time	0	1	2	3	4
Cash flow	(1,000)	50	100	800	250

2. Calculate the modified internal rate of return for the following cash flows using a reinvestment rate of 8.50%.

Time	0	1	2	3	4
Cash flow	(500)	30	500	50	100

3. Find the IRR(s) for the following cash flows:

Time	0	1	2	3	4
Cash flow	(5,000)	7,750	0	0	(2,800)

4. Calculate the Yield-To-Maturity on a 10-year bond with a 6.00% annual coupon when the price is 97.

5. Calculate the All-In-Cost for a $500,000,000 7-year bond with 7.50% annual coupon priced at 99 with a 1.5% fee and other costs of $250,000.

Due Diligence ANSWERS

1. NPV = (100.096)   IRR = 6.207%

2. MIRR = 11.801%

3. IRR = 1.593% and 28.778%

4. 6.416%

5. 7.990%

13. INTEREST RATES

WHERE DO INTEREST RATES COME FROM?

Interest rates reflect the interaction of the supply and demand for funds:

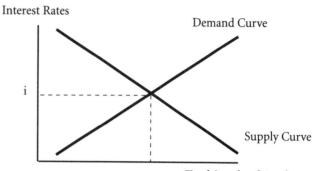

The above analysis is true from an economic standpoint, but it has limited use at an operational level. Instead, financial analysts think about interest rates as two elements; a return for lending somebody the money with no default risk (called the risk free rate) and a payment for any risk taken. The most important default risk is credit risk: the risk that the borrower will default.

Element 1: the benchmark rate

Investors expect a return for simply lending out their money, even if an investment is free of default risk. This element of their return reflects the pure "time value of money." The nearest measures we have of default-free interest rates in the US are the yields on US Government Treasury bills, bonds, and notes. It is inconceivable that the US government would go bankrupt. If it did we might as well go home!

> When the US government borrows, it issues bills, notes, and bonds

Presently the US Treasury issues eight different securities:

Treasury Bills	**13 week, 26 week, and 52 week maturities**
Treasury Notes	**2, 5, 10 year maturities**
Treasury Bonds	**30 year maturity (uncertain future)**

The terms **bill, note** and **bond** refer to the different maturities. Maturity means the time from original issue until the bill, note or bond is repaid. The most recently issued of each of these securities is called the "on the run" or "current" issue. The yields on these on-the-run issues and a few others provide the benchmark rates for other US dollar-denominated securities.

When the Treasury issues bills, notes and bonds

> What's short-term? Intermediate? Long-term?

The US Treasury issues Treasury bonds, notes, and bills on a regular schedule. Bills are short-term securities, notes are medium term securities and bonds are long-term securities. For other bonds, these terms are somewhat elastic and will vary from one conversation to another. For our purposes we will consider three to seven years to be intermediate term and beyond seven years to be long term.

Element 2: the risk part

Treasury securities have the lowest interest rates of any long-term securities. Investors are prepared to accept these low returns as they know Treasury securities are free of default risk. (However, they do have price risk if interest rates fluctuate.) Other issuers—corporations, other governments, and government agencies—are considered to have higher risk. The key risk that investors worry about is default risk. Default does not necessarily mean that the investor loses everything; it could mean a short delay in some of the payments, or receiving less than the expected value of the principal and interest payments. If investors perceive the risk of default is high, they will also demand a higher return.

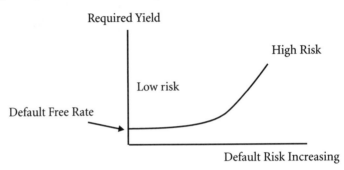

Initially the curve is relatively shallow, but it increases sharply at the point where an investment becomes **non-investment grade.**

WHAT'S THE CREDIT RATING?

The analysis of default risk is known as **credit analysis.** It is a huge business involving significant economies of scale. Organizations called rating agencies specialize in analyzing the default risk of bonds. When the rating agencies complete their work they usually communicate to the investing world using an abbreviated summary of their findings. These ratings are organized as a spectrum from lowest to highest risk. The ratings spectrum for the two largest agencies are shown below:

	Standard & Poor's	**Moody's Investors Services**
Lowest risk	AAA	Aaa
	AA	Aa
	A	A
	BBB	Baa
	BB	Ba
	B	B
	CCC	Caa
	CC	Ca
	C	C
Highest risk	D (in default)	

Fallen angels

Bonds which were issued as investment grade but have since fallen to junk status.

Risky business

Similar bonds, similar yields

Investors treat bonds with the same maturity and credit rating as close substitutes and expect their yields to be similar. Investment banks helping to issue new bonds with a specific maturity and credit rating will look at the yield of other bonds in the same category to calculate a suitable issue price. Commentators describe the status of bond markets in terms of bond yields for different maturities and credit ratings.

TALK THE TALK OF BONDS

Like interest rates, bond yields have two elements: 1) the benchmark rate, usually the government bond rate because it has the lowest default risk, and 2) the risk element. The starting point is the benchmark security in the market you are interested in. For US based bonds the benchmark is the US Treasury market. These securities have the lowest risk and largest, most liquid markets. In Japan the benchmark is the Japanese Government Bond (JGB), in the UK it is gilts, and so on.

The difference between the benchmark rate and a bond's yield is known as its **spread.** A bond's spread compensates the investor for taking the risk of investing in that particular security. The spread between different credit ratings and the benchmark rate tends to be more stable than absolute interest rates. Therefore, people in the financial markets talk about spreads rather than absolute interest rates. Let's take an example of how Joe, our trader friend, would discuss bonds:

> **EXAMPLE**
>
> Joe's client Ray Gwinnell from North Florida is interested in buying some five-year maturity, BBB rated corporate bonds. Joe turns to monitors on his desk and sees that the five-year Treasury note is yielding 5.00% and BBB rated bonds are yielding 6.30%.
>
> Joe calculates the spread: 6.30% − 5.00% = 1.30%. However, he tells Ray, "The current spread for BBB bonds is 130 basis points (bps). Spreads have been narrowing for the last week and we expect that to continue if the economic news continues to be favorable."
>
> A basis point is simply one hundredth of a percent.

How are maturity and interest rates linked?

Usually bonds with longer maturities have slightly higher interest rates or "yields" than bonds with shorter maturities. Several theories have been put forward put forward to explain why long-term bonds have higher interest rates than short-term bonds; we won't cover them in this book. A graph illustrating the relationship between yield and maturity for one credit rating is called the yield curve. Often several yield curves for different credit ratings are shown together:

Benchmark rate and risk element

Hint

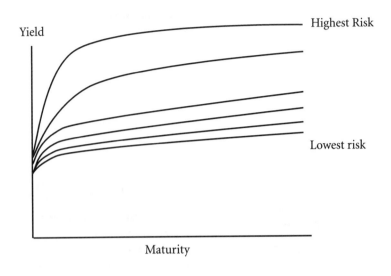

Investment grade: to be or not to be?

Bonds which have a credit rating of BBB (Standard & Poors) or Baa (Moody's Investor Services) or higher are considered investment grade bonds. The spectrum of yields for bonds rated between AAA and BBB is usually not wide. Below BBB or Baa yields start to increase dramatically. In the diagram above the lowest curve is for Treasurys, the next three lower yield curves are investment grade, the top two non-investment grade. Notice how the lower yield curves are much closer together.

Some financial institutions are limited in their investing in non-investment grade securities by rules in their articles or from regulatory agencies. Non-investment grade securities are known as **junk bonds**. Junk bond spreads widened dramatically following the Russian debt crisis in 1998.

Bonds make the grade—the investment grade

If they don't, they're junk

EXERCISE 31 ➤
Interest Rates and Yields

Interest Rates and Bond Yields

1. What is used as the benchmark rate in the US?

2. [ ] If a bond has a credit rating of CCC is it high or low risk?

3. [ ] If Joe, our trader, told you that BB spreads were 300 basis points and the treasury bond rate was 5.08% what should the yield of a BB rated bond be in the market?

4. Name the two major credit rating agencies.

5. [ ] If a B rated bond is yielding 5.98% will a BBB rated bond's yield be higher or lower?

14. SIMPLE INTEREST

Young and simple

For many short-term (under one-year) investments in the financial markets we use simple interest to calculate interest payments, present value (prices) and future values. Simple interest is exactly what it says it is—simple! It ignores interest on interest. Simple interest math is often referred to as **money market math.** Simple interest is primarily used in the money markets, therefore we will call simple interest rates **yields.** The basic formulas used are:

$$\text{Simple interest} \quad = \quad PV * \frac{yield * days}{360}$$

$$\text{Future Value} \quad = \quad PV * \left[1 + \frac{yield * days}{360}\right]$$

We don't want a whole year's yield

Simple interest calculations involve periods of less than one year, so you need to take a fraction of the yield. You can see from the above equations that the number of days divided by 360 is the proportion of the yield you want.

In the above equations time is measured in days and relates to how long you held the investment. Note as well that the "year" for calculations has 360 days. 360 is the convention for most, but not all, money markets around the world and is referred to as an "actual/360" system. Sometimes simple interest rates are abbreviated using actual/360 as SIR_{360}.

Debt bomb

When a major financial institution defaults, creating major shock waves throughout the financial system

EXAMPLE

Joe Angel is a bond salesman; he wants to calculate the simple interest due on an investment of €1,000 at 6% for 90 days. He first sets out the equation:

$$1,000 * \frac{0.06 * 90}{360} = 15$$

The interest owed to Joe would be €15.

Later the same day a client who is not very financially sophisticated asks Joe:
> "If I borrow €1,000,000 at 7% and repay it in 180 days, how much will I owe?"

Joe, who owes the client a favor, does the calculation for him:

$$1,000,000 * \left[1 + \left(\frac{0.07 * 180}{360}\right)\right] = 1,035,000$$

The future value formula is referred to as **"add-on-interest"** or **"interest at maturity."** Certificates of deposit, forward rate agreements, and foreign exchange swaps are all calculated using these formulas.

From the equation above, you can work out equations to find **simple interest yields** and **simple interest present value.**

$$\text{Present value} = \frac{FV}{\left(1 + \frac{yield * days}{360}\right)}$$

$$\text{Yield} = \left(\frac{FV}{PV} - 1\right) * \left(\frac{360}{days}\right)$$

EXERCISE 32 ➤
The Pitch

The pitch

The Pitch

1. What is the future value of €1,000,000 at a simple interest rate (SIR_{360}) of 6.00% in 90 days?

   $FV =$ [   ]

2. What is the future value to be received in 180 days if you invest USD50,000 at a simple interest rate of 5.85%? Use SIR_{360}.

   $FV =$ [   ]

3. What is the present value of $10,000,000 to be received in 270 days at a simple interest rate of 4.97%?

   $PV =$ [   ]

4. Calculate the total amount due at maturity on a $10,000,000 certificate of deposit (CD) when the term is 270 days and the interest rate is 5.83%.

   $FV =$ [   ]

5. Calculate the total amount due on a 90-day CD with a $100 million face value and a 6.15% rate.

   $FV =$ [   ]

A more accurate way

When you calculate the present value of short-term money market instruments you are dealing in **fractional periods**, i.e. periods of less than one year. Instead of using the simple interest equations above, a more accurate way would be to make the exponent in your present value equation a fraction:

$$PV = \frac{FV}{(1+r)^n} \quad \leftarrow \text{Exponent}$$

Fractional exponents

Fractional exponents are difficult to deal with unless you have a calculator. Equations involving them require significant computational effort. However, the money markets were around a long time before electronic calculators became widely used.

> Life before calculators did go on . . .

Avoiding calculation pain!

Not surprisingly, people sought to avoid this kind of calculation pain and turned to simple interest. It turns out that the results derived from using simple interest and compound interest are relatively close when the time period is short, as in money market investments.

Simple interest solved the computational headache, and didn't do too much violence to the mathematical result. Money market players adjust for the discrepancies between the two methods in their heads. As you might have guessed, tradition has stuck and this method of calculating interest in the money markets is widespread.

Golden handshake

Generous incentive given to an executive who agrees to leave the firm before their contract runs out. Golden handshakes are regularly used after takeovers.

> **EXAMPLE**
>
> Another of Joe's clients, Doug, calls up;
> > *"I have a certificate of deposit that will pay $1,045,000 in 90 days. What price will you give me for it?"*
>
> Joe looks at his Reuters screen; it shows 90-day certificate of deposit yields are 4.80%. He then makes the following calculation:
>
> $$PV = \frac{1,045,000}{\left(1 + \frac{0.0480*90}{360}\right)} = 1,032,608.70$$
>
> Joe buys a certificate of deposit for $1,035,000. It paid $1,050,000 90 days later. His return expressed in simple interest terms was:
>
> $$Yield = \left(\frac{1,050,000}{1,035,000} - 1\right) * \left(\frac{360}{90}\right) = 0.05797 = 5.797\%$$

If Joe had used compound interest to make his calculations

Here is what happens with these two examples if compound interest is used. We will retain the actual/360 convention of counting time.

Example 1:

$$PV = \frac{1,045,000}{(1+0.048)^{90/360}} = 1,032,823.16$$

Note that our compound interest answer is higher than our simple interest calculation by 214.

Example 2:

$$i = \left(\frac{FV}{PV}\right)^{\frac{1}{n}} - 1 = \left(\frac{1,050,000}{1,035,000}\right)^{\frac{360}{90}} = -1 = 5.924\%$$

Here our compound interest answer is higher by 0.127% or about 13 basis points.

E X E R C I S E   3 3 ➤
The Mandate

The Mandate

The Mandate

1. Calculate the simple interest due on a €250,000,000 loan for 92 days at 6.13%.

   Interest = _____

2. Calculate the total amount due at maturity on a 180-day, 6.10% €1,000,000 certificate of deposit.

   FV = _____

3. Calculate the present value of $200,000 due in 36 days at 5.22%.

   PV = _____

4. You have $10 million to invest for 180 days and think that an investment in a certificate of deposit (CD) offering a 5.90% interest rate is a good idea, so you buy it. Sixty days later, you find that you need the money and want to sell the CD in the secondary market. At that time the rate on 120-day CDs is 6.10%. What will you receive if you sell it then?

   There are two steps to getting the answer to this question:

   Step 1: Calculate the amount due at maturity

   Amount due = _____

   Step 2: Find the present value 60 days from now of the value at maturity.

   PV = _____

The Mandate - continued

5. You invested €1,000,000. After 180 days it was worth €1,029,313. What simple interest rate did you earn? Use SIR_{360}.

Interest rate =

6. You buy a 150-day CD for $1,000,000. The contract rate on the CD is 6.78%. After 30 days you sell the CD. At that point, 120-day CDs are yielding 6.47%. Use SIR_{360}.

What price did you sell your CD for?

Price =

What return did you receive for the 30 days you held the CD? Use SIR_{360}.

Return =

Hit the phones

Hit the Phones! Summary

1. The financial markets use simple interest for securities that have maturities of less than one year.

2. Simple interest is interest calculated only on the original investment. It excludes interest on interest.

3. There are different market conventions when it comes to deciding how many days to use as a full year. Check the practice for the particular security or market.

4. The important simple interest equations include:

Simple interest amount = $\qquad PV * \dfrac{yield * days}{360}$

Future Value = $\qquad PV * \left[1 + \dfrac{yield * days}{360}\right]$

Present Value = $\qquad \dfrac{FV}{\left(1 + \dfrac{yield * days}{360}\right)}$

Yield = $\qquad \left[\dfrac{FV}{PV} - 1\right]\left[\dfrac{360}{Days}\right]$

5. Time is measured in days.

15. NOMINAL AND EFFECTIVE INTEREST RATES

So far, you've seen bonds with annual coupons and interest rates compounded annually. This is true of Eurobonds and bonds issued by many European governments. Some products in the financial markets have payments that are semi-annual such as US government bonds. Still others such as mortgages have quarterly and monthly payments. A few are even bi-weekly. Generally there are two rules that determine the compounding frequency.

- **The number of times interest is compounded follows the number of times coupons are paid in a year.**
- **Zero coupon bonds follow the same compounding convention as paying coupon securities in the same market. For example, zero coupon Eurobonds use annual compounding, while zero coupon US Treasury bonds (strips) use semi-annual compounding.**

Annual or semi-annual?

Semi-annual coupons probably resulted from investors wanting to be paid sooner. Gilts (UK government bonds), Treasurys (US government bonds), Japanese government Bonds, US corporates, US agencies, US municipals and more all have semi-annual coupons.

Bearer bonds

With bearer bonds, possession is 100% of the law

Eurobonds are often in bearer form, which means they are like cash: the person who physically holds the bond owns it. They have physical coupons attached. The process of paying, gathering up and providing custody for all these little pieces of paper is costly and as a result the bonds are designed to make these cumbersome payments infrequently, i.e., annually.

Nominal and effective interest rates

Step into the financial markets' traditions and learn some terms

OK, prepare to be confused. The actual concept of nominal and effective interest rates is pretty simple. However, like most financial concepts born out of tradition, expediency rather than logic drove the concept of the nominal interest rates.

When the compounding of an investment's interest is more than once per year, the interest rate quoted is called the **nominal rate.**

Ankle biter

A stock whose total market worth is less than $500 million

EXAMPLE

An investor who earns 4.50% every six months earns **more** than 9.00% over the year because of the **interest earned on the first interest payment.** However, in the markets the investment's yield is quoted as "9.00% yield with semi-annual compounding." The 9.00% is a **nominal** yield.

For instance, 9.00% with semi-annual compounding means 9.00% ÷ 2 = 4.50% per half-year. However, the result of two half years at 4.50% per half year is:

$$9.2025\% = (1 + 0.045) * (1 + 0.045) - 1$$

9.2025% is called the **Effective Rate.** The effective rate is the mathematically correct yield. However, the convention in the financial markets is to talk about the yield as "9.00% semi-annual."

Using 9.00% as a nominal rate for different compounding frequencies gives us the following results:

Nominal Rate	Frequency	Per year	Effective Rate
9.00%	Annual	1	9.0000%
9.00%	Semi-annual	2	9.2025%
9.00%	Quarterly	4	9.3083%
9.00%	Monthly	12	9.3807%
9.00%	Bi-weekly	26	9.4004%
9.00%	Weekly	52	9.4089%
9.00%	Daily	365	9.4162%
9.00%	Hourly	8,760	9.4174%
9.00%	Continuous	–	9.4174%

Key point

The more frequently interest payments occur, the higher the effective rate. The equation relating nominal and effective rates is:

$$\text{Effective Rate} = \left[1 + \frac{\text{Nominal Rate}}{\text{frequency}}\right]^{\text{frequency}} - 1$$

$$\text{Nominal Rate} = \left[(\text{Effective Rate} + 1)^{\frac{1}{\text{frequency}}} - 1\right] * \text{frequency}$$

It is important that you have a thorough understanding of this concept before you move on. Many people find it very confusing.

Nominal? Effective? You must be able to sling these terms around

Using the HP-12C

To convert from a nominal rate with P payments per year to an effective rate Press

NOM **ENTER** P **÷** 1 **+** P **yˣ** 1 **−** .

For 9% with semi-annual compounding

.09 **ENTER** 2 **÷** 1 **+** 2 **yˣ** 1 **−** = 9.203%.

For 9% with quarterly compounding

.09 **ENTER** 4 **÷** 1 **+** 4 **yˣ** 1 **−** = 9.308%.

EXERCISE 34 ➤
The Pitch

The pitch

The Pitch

1. Fill in the blanks in the following table

Nominal Rate	Effective Rate	Compounding
8.00%		2
9.00%		4
	8.50%	12
	8.90%	2
8.00%	8.30%	

(You need to use trial and error to solve the last problem)

2. Convert the following from nominal rates to effective rates. Calculate your answer to four places.

Nominal rate	Compounding	Effective rate
6.50%	2	
6.50%	4	
7.50%	1	
7.50%	4	
8.00%	2	
8.00%	4	
8.00%	1	

3. Convert the following from effective rates to nominal rates. Calculate your answers to four places.

Effective rate	Compounding	Nominal rate
6.33%	1	
6.33%	2	
6.33%	12	
4.85%	2	
4.85%	4	

> Divide a semi-annual coupon by 2 to get the cash flow

Calculating the yield of semi-annual coupon bonds

Calculating the yield on a bond that pays its interest in two coupon payments per year is slightly different from what we have done before. Try an easy example first.

EXAMPLE

Suppose you had a 1-year bond with a $100 face value and a 10% coupon rate paid semi-annually. The coupon payment is split into two payments of $5 each, paid six months apart. If you could buy it for 100 your cash flows would look like this:

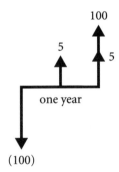

Drawing the diagram is especially helpful for questions like these.

Hint

Different compounding different periods

When analyzing a bond that pays its coupons semi-annually, we restate the problem so that the period in our cash flow diagram is six months rather than one year as in earlier sections of this book. Accordingly, the end of the year is shown as being the end of period two above.

Next find the IRR of the cash flows using the TVM keys where:

TVM KEYS

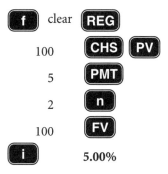

Our answer is that the investor's yield is 5% per six months. People don't talk about the yield as 5% every six months. Instead they will quote the **nominal rate.** To get the nominal rate we simply multiply the yield by the number of payments made in the year, in this case two.

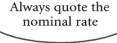

Always quote the nominal rate

The Yield-To-Maturity is: 5% * 2 = 10% (with semi-annual compounding). This yield of 10% is a **nominal** yield and will normally be expressed as "10% s.a."

EXAMPLE

Try a more complicated situation. Calculate the yield on a 9.00% coupon bond (paid semi-annually) with a five year maturity and a price of 98.

First draw the diagram:

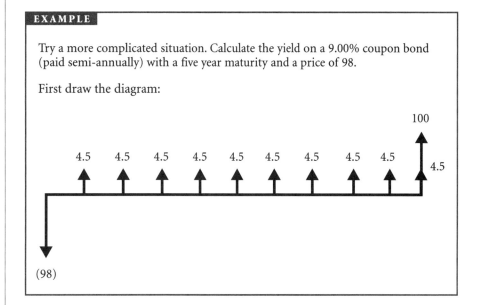

EXAMPLE - continued

Next calculate the IRR using the TVM keys:

TVM KEYS

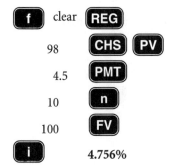

f	clear	REG
98	CHS	PV
4.5	PMT	
10	n	
100	FV	
i		**4.756%**

Now calculate the nominal rate:

4.756 * 2 = 9.512% (with semi-annual compounding) = Yield-to-Maturity (YTM).

E X E R C I S E   3 5 ➤
The Mandate

The Mandate

The Mandate

1. What is the Yield-To-Maturity of a 5-year 8.00% coupon bond (paid semi-annually) selling for 99?

    YTM =

2. Calculate the Yield-To-Maturity on a 10-year 6.50% coupon bond (paid semi-annually) selling at 103.50.

    YTM =

3. Calculate the All-In-Cost for a 3-year, 7.00% coupon bond (paid semi-annually) with a price of 99.50 and issue costs of 1.00%.

    YTM =

4. Calculate the YTM of a 6-year, 7.20% coupon bond (paid monthly) at a price of 102.

    YTM =

Hit the phones

Hit the Phones! Summary

1. Some products in the financial markets pay coupons more than once a year. If a security pays interest more than once a year, you need to take into account the compounding effect.

2. The number of times interest is compounded follows the number of times coupons are paid in a year.

3. **Bearer bonds** are like cash. The person who holds a bearer bond owns it.

4. A **nominal interest** rate is the simple addition of the coupons described as a % of par, paid in one year.

5. An **effective interest** rate is the mathematically correct IRR for an investment.

6. The equations used to convert between nominal and effective rates are:

Effective Rate = $\left[1 + \dfrac{\text{Nominal Rate}}{\text{frequency}}\right]^{\text{frequency}} - 1$

Nominal Rate = $\left[\left(\text{Effective Rate} + 1\right)^{\frac{1}{\text{frequency}}} - 1\right] * \text{frequency}$

7. When you are drawing a diagram for a bond which pays coupons more than once a year, make sure you use payment periods and not years when illustrating your coupon cash flows.

16. COMPARING BONDS

You have the tools, now follow the rules

As an investor, you want to choose the bond with the highest YTM. Your choices are:

- **3-year Eurobond with 9.00% coupon (paid annually) at a price of 102**
- **3-year Corporate bond with 9.50% coupon (paid semi-annually) at a price of 104.**

Which bond do you choose?

Step 1: Calculate the YTM for each bond

Eurobond:

TVM KEYS

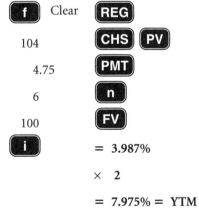

f	Clear	REG
102		CHS PV
9		PMT
3		n
100		FV
i		**8.221% = YTM**

Corporate:

TVM KEYS

f	Clear	REG
104		CHS PV
4.75		PMT
6		n
100		FV
i		**= 3.987%**
		× 2
		= 7.975% = YTM

The two rates you just calculated are not directly comparable since the Eurobond's YTM of 8.221% is calculated with annual compounding (therefore it is an effective rate) and the corporate's YTM of 7.975% with semi-annual compounding. You should write:

■ **Eurobond**   **8.221% (annual)**
■ **Corporate**   **7.975% (semi-annual)**

to help make the distinction between the two rates.

Get out your crystal ball

In practice you are supposed to know!

In practice, unfortunately, you are supposed to know from the context, i.e., the market in which the bonds trade, whether the rate quoted is an annual rate or a rate with semi-annual compounding, etc.

In this case, you would be expected to know that Eurobonds normally have annual coupons and their yields are stated as effective rates.

Warning

When comparing yields, check the basis

In order to compare the two bonds' yields, first we need to make sure they are on the same "basis." If one yield is semi-annual and one yield is effective, we must first convert one of them so that either both have nominal or both have effective rates.

The easiest way is to convert both bonds to effective rates, i.e., annual rates. Convert the corporate semi-annual rate to an effective rate using the following equation:

$$\text{Effective Rate} = \left(1 + \frac{7.975\%}{2}\right)^2 - 1 = 8.134\%$$

or, using the calculator:

.07975 **ENTER** 2 **÷** 1 **+** 2 **yˣ** 1 **−** = 8.134%

Now you can compare

Making money

When to Convert Interest Rates

A Geneva-based fixed income fund manager might be accustomed to analyzing prospective bonds using effective rates. The majority of investments would likely be in continental European sovereigns (government bonds) and Eurobonds, which pay coupons annually and are quoted in the financial markets at effective rates (rates with annual compounding).

On this basis the comparison would be:

	Effective (annual) Rate
Eurobond	8.221%
Corporate Domestic	8.134%

The Eurobond would get the nod as it has a higher effective yield.

On the other hand, the fixed income manager for Metropolitan Life (a US life Insurance company) would most likely have a portfolio of domestic US corporate bonds, government agency bonds and US Treasury bonds, all of which have semi-annual coupons and semi-annual compounding. In such a case, the better comparison would be to convert the Eurobonds' annual YTM to an equivalent YTM with semi-annual compounding.

EXERCISE 36 ➤
The Pitch

The pitch

The Pitch

1. Calculate the yield on two 5-year bonds and compare them. Which bond would you invest in?
   - **Bond A:** **6.00% coupon (annual) at 98.00** ❑
   - **Bond B:** **6.10% coupon (semi-annual) at 99.50** ❑

2. Compare 10-year bonds C and D in terms of Yield-To-Maturity, expressed as effective rates. Which bond would you pick?
   - **Bond C:** **8.00% coupon (annual), priced at 104** ❑
   - **Bond D:** **5.75% coupon (semi-annual), priced at 89** ❑

3. Calculate the All-In-Cost for bonds E and F. Both have 5-year maturities and par values of $500 million. Which bond would you issue?
   - **Bond E:** **6.75% coupon (annual), priced at 101, 1 7/8% fee, and other issuance costs of $200,000.** ❑
   - **Bond F:** **6.50% coupon (semi-annual), priced at 98, 0.65% fee, and other issuance costs of $100,000.** ❑

4. Calculate the All-In-Costs of bonds G and H. Both have 10-year maturities and par values of $750,000,000. Which bond would you issue?
   - **Bond G:** **7.125% coupon (annual), priced at 100.5, 2% fee and other issuance costs of $300,000.** ❑
   - **Bond H:** **7.00% coupon (semi-annual), priced at 99, 0.70% fee and other issuance costs of $250,000.** ❑

Nominal to nominal

More on nominal rates

Sometimes you will want to convert directly from one nominal rate to another without caring about the effective rate. Sales and trading professionals on swap desks make such conversions routinely throughout the day as they tailor swap contracts to client needs.

EXAMPLE

Convert 8.00% quarterly to a semi-annual rate. First convert the quarterly rate to an effective rate and then convert your effective rate to a semi-annual rate.

Quarterly Rate	→	Effective Rate	→	Semi-annual Rate

Step 1: Convert your 8.00% quarterly rate to an effective rate:

$$\left(1 + \frac{0.08}{4}\right)^4 - 1 \; = \; \text{Effective Rate} \; = \; 0.08243$$

Step 2: Convert your effective rate to a new nominal rate:

$$\left[(0.08243 + 1)^{1/2} - 1\right] * 2 \; = \text{Semi-annual Rate} \; = \; 0.08080 \; = \; 8.080\%$$

Alternatively, you can use your calculator and do it in one step:

.08 [ENTER] 4 [÷] 1 [+] 4 [yˣ] .5 [yˣ]

1 [−] 2 [x] = 8.080%

A short cut

An equation for the pros

If you don't do this very much, convert the first nominal rate into an effective rate and then to another nominal rate. If you are pretty confident with the above equations and are likely to be making these calculations frequently, here's a short cut to use if your calculator is not handy.

$$\begin{array}{c}\text{New} \\ \text{Nominal Rate}\end{array} = \left[\left(1 + \frac{\text{Old Nominal Rate}}{\text{Old frequency}}\right)^{\text{Old frequency}/\text{New frequency}} - 1\right] * \text{New frequency}$$

The Mandate

Hit the phones

The Mandate

1. Convert the following rates:

   a.   8.00% (sa)   =   [   ]   quarterly

   b.   7.22% (ann)   =   [   ]   sa

   c.   6.88% (monthly)   =   [   ]   sa

   d.   7.03% (quarterly)   =   [   ]   sa

   e.   7.19% (sa)   =   [   ]   quarterly

2. Convert the following rates:

   a.   7.00% (sa)   =   [   ]   quarterly

   b.   7.00% (sa)   =   [   ]   monthly

   c.   7.00% (sa)   =   [   ]   daily

   d.   7.00% (sa)   =   [   ]   annually

Hit the Phones! Summary

1. If you compare the yields of two bonds, make sure they use the same compounding frequency.

2. Different markets use different conventions. Always check the market convention and ensure all your yields meet the market practice.

3. If you convert to the yearly effective rate first, you are less likely to make mistakes.

17. HOLDING PERIOD YIELD

Be HaPpY— calculate HPY

This section develops the concept of the Holding Period Yield (HPY) which is an application of the concept of the Modified Internal Rate of Return (MIRR). The HPY is calculated for the period during which the bond is held and requires an estimate of the selling price of the bond at the end of the holding period and the reinvestment rate(s) of the coupons received during the holding period. Here is an example:

EXAMPLE

You buy a 5-year, 8.00% annual coupon bond from the original issue date at par (100% of its value at maturity). After two years your trader friend Joe buys it from you at a yield of 8.10%. During the two years, you reinvested the coupons at 7.50% at your investment bank Lynch Barney.

Step 1:   Draw the cash flow diagram.

Selling Price

8

8

(100)

Step 2:   Calculate the selling price for a 3-year bond with an 8.00% coupon rate at a yield of 8.10%.

TVM KEYS

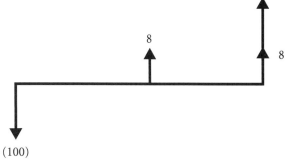

f Clear	**REG**	
8.10	**i**	
8	**PMT**	
3	**n**	
100	**FV**	
FV	= (99.743)	

Step 3: Find the future value of the intermediate cash flow at the end of year one using the reinvestment of 7.50%.

$$8.00 * (1 + 0.075) = 8.60$$

Step 4: Add the future value of the coupons to the selling price and draw the new cash flow diagram.

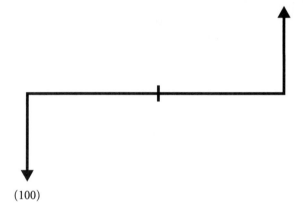

+ 8.600
+ 8.000
+ 99.743
= 116.343

(100)

Step 5: Solve for the holding period yield.

TVM KEYS

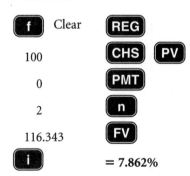

f Clear	REG	
100	CHS	PV
0	PMT	
2	n	
116.343	FV	
i	= 7.862%	

Bottom fisher

An investor who looks for stocks which have hit rock bottom

EXERCISE 38 ➤
The Pitch

The pitch

The Pitch

1. You buy a 30-year 7.25% coupon bond (paid annually) at 98 and sell it three years later at 101. During the three years you reinvest the coupons at 6.90%. What is your holding period yield?

2. You buy a 15-year zero coupon bond at a yield of 8.22%. Four years later you sell the bond at a yield of 7.18%. What is your holding period yield?

3. You buy a 10-year 6.00% coupon bond (paid annually) at 103. Two years later you sell the bond at a yield of 6.80%. You reinvest your coupons at 6.20% during the two years. What is your holding period yield?

4. You buy a 30-year 7.00% coupon bond (paid annually) at a yield of 6.90%. You hold the bond for five years, during which you reinvest coupons at 6.50%. At the end of the five years you sell the bond at a yield of 6.45%. What is your holding period yield?

5. You buy a 7-year, 5.50% coupon bond (paid annually) at a yield of 5.75%. Three years later you sell it at a yield of 6.03%. During the three years you reinvest coupons at 6.00%. What is your holding period yield?

18. BOND MATH

Until now we have dealt with bullet bonds on coupon dates. These bonds are easy to calculate because you're using whole time periods without any fractions. But what if there are fractional time periods? For instance, what if the bond pays one coupon per year, but the next payment is due 5 months from now?

Most bond trading and investing activity takes place in the secondary markets and therefore trades usually fall in the middle of a coupon period. We need more power to calculate prices and yields in these situations.

THE GEOGRAPHY OF THE COUPON PERIOD

We need to know where in the period we are when we calculate prices and yields. There are several ways to measure these fractional periods. These methods are called **Day Count Conventions.** Each method counts the number of days in the coupon period and the days between dates in a special way. The popular methods are called **Actual/Actual** and **30/360.**

Actual/Actual counts the days in the coupon period by calculating the actual number of days that the period contains for the denominator and the actual number of days since the last coupon as the numerator. With Actual/Actual a half-year may contain 181, 182, 183 or 184 days depending on which dates are used in the calculation.

The **30/360** day count convention assumes that all months have thirty days. Thus February gets an added two days in non-leap years and January, March, May, July, August, October and December lose their last day. With 30/360 a half-year always contains 180 days.

You must enter dates in the calculator in one of two different formats: D.MY or M.DY. D.MY is the "international" or "military" format. It puts the day of the month first, followed by the number of the month and then the year.

March 31, 2005 = 31.032005.

Notice where the decimal point goes. Give the calculator the format it expects!

The M.DY format puts the month first, then the day and year.
March 31, 2005 = 3.312005.

Again, notice the placement of the decimal point and do what the calculator expects!

We will use the M.DY format throughout the exercises in this book.

The HP-12C calculates the days between two dates using the ⟨ΔDYS⟩ key. Find this blue key just above the ⟨ENTER⟩ key. To calculate the days between March 15, 2005 and September 15, 2005 press the following.

3.152005 ⟨ENTER⟩

9.152005 ⟨g⟩

⟨ΔDYS⟩ = 184

The answer, 184, is the actual number of days between the two dates.

To find the number of days using the 30/360 day count convention, press the

[X ↔ Y] key to see that there are 180 days (ignoring March 31, May 31, July 31 and August 31).

EXERCISE 39 ➤
The Pitch

The pitch

The Pitch

Use the calculator to determine the number of days between the following dates using both Actual/Actual and 30/360 day count conventions.

Begin Date	End Date
January 15, 2007	June 12, 2007
June 6, 2004	December 6, 2004
February 15, 2004	August 15, 2004

You can also find the future date if you know the starting date and the number of days by using the [DATE] key (in blue on the [CHS] key two up from the [ENTER] key). For example, find the future date if you start on July 10, 2004 and add 151 days:

7.102004   [ENTER]

151   [g]

[DATE]   12,08,2004   3

The future date is December 8, 2004 and it is a Wednesday. The calculator begins the week on Monday, i.e., Monday = 1, Tuesday = 2, Wednesday = 3, etc.

EXERCISE 40 ➤
The Pitch

The pitch

The Pitch

Calculate the future (or past) dates for the following.

Start Dates	Change in Days
January 4, 2006	210
March 12, 2003	400
June 18, 2004	−180

DIFFERENT CONVENTIONS FOR DIFFERENT BONDS

Different bonds use different conventions for day count and for coupon payments. Here are some examples.

	Annual Coupons	Semi-Annual Coupons
Actual/Actual	European Sovereign Bonds	US Treasury Bonds and Notes
30/360	Eurobonds	US Corporates, Agencys, Municipals

The HP-12C's BOND keys are designed to do calculations for Actual/Actual day count and semi-annual coupons, i.e., for US Treasury bonds and notes. This book focuses on these instruments. The results you would get if you used the calculator's BOND keys for 30/360 day count and semi-annual coupons are close but not exact. Other HP calculators can deal with these other bond categories.

How a bond is priced

The value of a bond is the present value of its cash flows. But if a bond is sold between coupon dates, calculating its value is somewhat complicated. First, let's define several terms. The present value of the bond will be called the **"Dirty Price"** or the **"Full Price."** It is the amount you have to pay if you buy the bond. If you are in the middle of a coupon period, however, the calculation of the dirty price will involve fractional exponents.

The dirty price is separated into two parts:

1. the **"Clean Price"** (**"Flat Price,"** or most commonly, just the **Price**)

2. **Accrued Interest.**

   Dirty price = clean price + accrued interest
   Clean price = dirty price − accrued interest

Time is measured to the day of the settle or settlement, i.e., when the bond is paid for and title changes.

Let's get accrued interest out of the way first. Accountants need to calculate how much of a bond's interest coupon is attributable to different reporting periods. A bond that pays an annual coupon each June 30 will have accrued half its coupon as of December 31 and accountants will want to attribute that half to the year just ending. The second half of the coupon goes to the next year upcoming. Since the conventions for allocating the coupons to different accounting periods was developed before powerful calculators were available, you shouldn't be surprised that the method uses simple interest.

At any point the accrued interest on a bond is proportional to the fraction of the coupon period that has elapsed. The formula for accrued interest is

$$\text{Accrued interest} = \frac{\text{Days since last coupon}}{\text{Days in coupon period}} * \text{Coupon amount}.$$

You can see that the day count convention you use will cause slight differences in the numbers that go into the fraction on the left. Actual/Actual will give slightly different answers from 30/360.

Let's do an example of pricing a two-year US Treasury note. Price the 6.00% T-note due 15 August 2005 to settle on 30 October 2003 at a yield of 6.20%.

First draw a diagram of the cash flows.

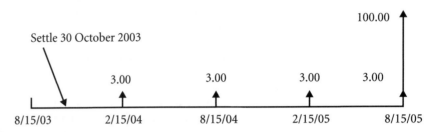

Basis = 184 days
76 days/108 days

There are 184 days in the coupon period (called the **Basis**). Seventy-six days have elapsed between the beginning of the period and the settlement date, and 108 days remain until the next coupon. For purposes of calculating the present value of the cash flows, the interest rate per half-year is 3.10%. The present value calculation is as follows.

$$PV = \text{Dirty Price} = 3/(1+.0310)^{(108/184)} + 3/(1+.0310)^{(1+108/184)}$$
$$+ 3/(1+.0310)^{(2+108/184)} + 103/(1+.0310)^{(3+108/184)}$$
$$= 2.95 + 2.86 + 2.77 + 92.32 = 100.893$$

Accrued interest in this case is

$$1.239 = \frac{76}{184} \times 3.00$$

The clean price is the present value (or dirty price) minus accrued interest, so

$$\text{Clean price} = 100.893 - 1.239 = 99.654$$

Calculating the clean price, accrued interest and dirty price is very easy using the HP-12C. Here is how to find these.

1. Enter the coupon rate (annual) in **PMT**.

2. Enter the yield in **i**.

3. Input the settle date and press **ENTER**.

4. Input the maturity date.

5. Press **f** **PRICE**. The answer is the clean price.

6. Press the **X ↔ Y** key. The answer is the accrued interest.

7. Press **+**. The answer is the dirty price.

EXAMPLE

Example using the 6.00% due 15 August 2005 to settle on 30 October 2003 at a yield of 6.20%.

6 **PMT**

6.2 **i**

10.302003 **ENTER**

8.152005

f **PRICE** 99.654

X ↔ Y 1.239

+ 100.893

EXERCISE 41 ➤
The Mandate

The pitch

The Mandate

Find the prices of the following bonds and notes assuming a settle date of 15 October 2003.

6.50% due 8/15/2007 at a yield of 6.02%
5 3/8% due 2/15/2031 at a yield of 4.80%
14.00% due 11/15/2011 at a yield of 5.10%

Calculating the yield given a price

The algebraic calculation of the price above was tedious but doable. The calculation of the yield given the price is done by searching and is considerably more burdensome if you do not use the calculator's functions. Here are the calculator steps to calculate the yield given the clean price.

Remember to use the clean price when communicating with the calculator.

Let's calculate the yield on the same note on October 30, 2003 if the clean price is 96-12, i.e., 96 12/32% of par. The price converts to 96.375. Here are the steps.

6 **PMT** 96.375 **PV** 10.302003 **ENTER**

8.152005 **f** **YTM** = **8.206%**

EXERCISE 42 ➤
The Mandate

The pitch

The Mandate

Calculate the yields of the following bonds and notes to settle 15 October 2003.

6.50% due 8/15/2007 at a price of 99.50
5 3/8% due 2/15/2031 at a price of 96.00
14.00% due 11/15/2011 at a price of 140.75

19. CONSTANTLY GROWING CASH FLOWS

You can take the concept of discounting cash flows using an interest rate and also use it to value a company. The idea is the value of a company is the value of its future cash flows discounted to today. This is called the **discounted cash flow valuation approach** (DCF). We will not cover it in detail here apart from an interesting problem it generates.

The value of a business is its future cash flows

Businesses theoretically continue forever, so an infinitely large analysis would be required to calculate a present value of all the cash flows. In practical terms, you simply select a time horizon that is short enough to make the DCF analysis manageable and long enough to exploit any special insights that the analyst has regarding the company's prospects, strategy, competitors or regulatory environment. Beyond this time horizon you can use an equation which calculates the present value of a series of cash flows growing forever at a steady percentage rate.

> Boil forever down to a manageable time

Today

Steadily growing cash flows to infinity and beyond . . .

Steady growth rate

A very popular model

> Growing to infinity and beyond

Beyond the initial time horizon, the DCF approach assumes all the future cash flows grow at a constant rate from year to year, out to infinity. When the cash flows are growing at a constant percentage rate, the company is said to have reached its **"steady state phase."**

You need to calculate the present value of these cash flows to infinity. Algebraically it looks like this in the situation where the steady state begins now.

$$PV = \frac{CF_1}{(1+i)} + \frac{CF_1(1+g)}{(1+i)^2} + \frac{CF_1(1+g)^2}{(1+i)^3} + \ldots\ldots\ldots\ldots$$

CF_1 is the cash flow in year 1, i is the appropriate interest rate and g is the growth rate in the cash flow received from one year to the next.

Chinese wall

An imaginary barrier between the advisory, research, and corporate finance departments and the sales & trading departments of an investment bank

The sum of an infinite geometric series

This calculation is the sum of an "infinite geometric series." From algebra you know the sum of an infinite geometric series is calculated by the following equation:

$$\text{Sum} = \frac{\text{First Term}}{1 - \text{Common Ratio}}$$

In this case the first term is $\dfrac{CF_1}{(1+i)}$

and the common ratio from one term to the next is $\dfrac{(1+g)}{(1+i)}$

Substituting this in the equation above results in:

$$PV = \text{Sum} = \frac{\dfrac{CF_1}{(1+i)}}{1 - \dfrac{(1+g)}{(1+i)}} \text{, and this simplifies to } PV = \frac{CF_1}{i - g}$$

This simplification is of enormous help when calculating the value of the cash flows beyond your initial time horizon. The equation above is frequently used to help value cash flows stretching out to infinity.

Don't worry too much if you didn't follow the algebra above. Just remember the equation.

Algebra to the rescue!

EXAMPLE

Aunt Agatha, a distant relative, leaves you 1,000 shares of Florida Amusement Parks Inc. You check out the stock on Bloomberg. It shows the company's next dividend will be $4.00. You read some research on Florida Amusement which tells you its dividend is expected to grow at a steady 4% in the future. Using a discount rate of 10%, what is your estimate of Florida Amusement's stock value?

$$PV = \text{Sum} = \frac{\$4.00}{0.10 - 0.04} = \$66.67$$

EXERCISE 43 ➤
The Pitch

The pitch

The Pitch

1. What is the present value of an infinite stream of cash flows that grow after year 1 at 5.00%? The cash flow in year 1 is €120 and the required interest rate is 10.00%.

    PV = [   ]

2. Calculate the present value of an infinite cash flow stream that begins with AUS 150,000 in year 1 and grows at 3.75%. Use an interest rate of 8.95%.

    PV = [   ]

3. Calculate the present value of an infinite cash flow stream that begins with CDN 20 million in year 1 and grows at 2.90% per year. Use an interest rate of 9.75%.

    PV = [   ]

4. **A harder question.**

    Your cash flow forecast is in the table below:

Time	Cash flow
0	0
1	0
2	0
3	100
4	104
etc. forever	Growing at 4%

    Your required interest rate is 10%. What is the present value of the cash flows?

    PV = [   ]

Using financial math to value a company

Now you can pool your knowledge so far to estimate the value of a company by using its forecasted cash flows.

EXAMPLE

A friend of yours calls up and tells you she has a business proposal:

> *"I want to purchase a restaurant in New York City. Will you look at my forecasts and tell me what you think?"*

You have known this friend a long time. She is pretty competent at forecasting and extremely good at cooking. You reply

> *"Tell me your cash flow forecast."*

> *"No problem,"*

she replies,

> *"I expect the business to require an investment of $100,000 now, $50,000 next year, then generate a positive cash flow of $25,000, $60,000 and $100,000 over the next three years. At the end of year five the cash flow will be $120,000. I estimate that the annual cash flows will grow at 5% after year 5."*

You then ask,

> *"OK, tell me what your cost of capital is."*

She says,

> *"11%."*

What is a fair price for the restaurant business?

Step 1: First diagram the cash flows:

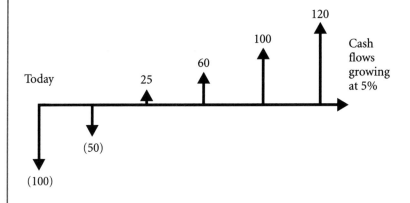

Step 2: Calculate the terminal value of the cash flows after Year 4.

$$PV_4 = \frac{CF_1}{i-g} = \frac{120}{0.11 - 0.05} = 2,000.00.$$

Buying a restaurant

Cash cow

A company that generates a steady stream of positive cash flows

Warning

Making money

EXAMPLE

Step 3: Add the terminal value as of the end of Year 4 to the cash flow in Year 4. Beware, it's a common error to add it to year 5.

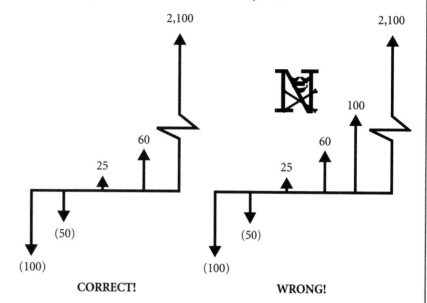

CORRECT!

WRONG!

Step 4: Calculate the net present value at 11% = $1,302.452

You can now call your friend and tell her a fair price for the business would be $1.3 million.

Note that you cannot calculate the IRR using these cash flows (plus any investment amount today) since the terminal value itself depends on the discount rate you are using. If you do want to calculate an IRR, it must be done by trial and error.

EXERCISE 44 ➤
The Mandate

The Mandate

The Mandate

1. Calculate the present value of an infinite series of cash flows growing at 3.10% where the first cash flow received at the end of year 1 is 2,000 and the required interest rate is 12.50%.

    PV = ☐

2. Calculate the present value at time 0 of an infinite series of cash flows that starts at the end of time period 11 with a value of 250 and grows at 2.50%. Use 10.60% as the required interest rate.

    PV = ☐

3. Calculate the present value using a 11.00% interest rate of an infinite series of cash flows that begins at 100 at the end of year 1 and declines at 5% per year.

    PV = ☐

The Mandate - continued

4. You estimate the cash flows from an investment as shown below. Calculate the present value today at 9.30%.

Time	Cash flow
0	(1,000)
1	(500)
2	50
3	100
4	105
etc. forever	Growing at 5%

PV = _____

5. Calculate the present value today of an energy saving investment that has the cash flows below. Use 9.00% as the required interest rate.

Time	Cash flow
0	(500,000)
1	10,000
2	21,000
etc. forever	Growth of 3%

PV = _____

6. **The stretch question!**

Use the information in question 5 above and calculate the IRR of the investment. You will have to do this by trial and error using different interest rates.

IRR = _____

Hit the phones

Hit the Phones! Summary

1. One way of valuing a company, called the Discounted Cash Flow (DCF) method, is to calculate the present value of its expected future cash flows.

2. Financial analysts performing a DCF valuation will forecast a company's cash flows until the business reaches a **steady state** of growth. They then calculate the value of the business in perpetuity using the growing perpetuity equation:

$$PV = \frac{CF_1}{i - g}$$

3. When you are using the above equation remember to add your answer to the end of the **previous** year.

Due Diligence

1. [ ]   Calculate the interest due after 91 days on a loan of $500 million when the simple interest rate (SIR_{360}) is 7.04%.

2. [ ]   What is the price of a two-year bond with a 6.00% coupon (paid semi-annually) when the yield is 7.04% (SA)?

3. [ ]   What is the present value of a cash flow stream whose first cash flow at the end of Year 1 is $50,000 and grows thereafter at 4.00% forever? Use an interest rate of 9.50%.

4. [ ]   Calculate the yield (with semi-annual compounding) for a 4-year bond with a 7.00% coupon (paid semi-annually) and a price of 104.25.

5. [ ]   What is the price today of a certificate of deposit that pays $1,045,000 in 45 days? Use a simple interest rate of 7.40% (SIR_{360}).

Due Diligence ANSWERS

1. 8,897,777.78

2. (98.091)

3. 909,090.01

4. 5.794% (SA)

5. 1,035,422.34

THE UNDERWRITING

Congratulations!

You made it through the book. Here's your chance to prove you are capable to start working in the capital markets. Take some time to review any areas you are uncomfortable with.

Take the assignment in a quiet place. You should allow yourself no more than one hour to complete all the questions.

Good luck.

The Underwriting

Archer Inc. is trying to decide whether to invest $500 million in Target Co., a leading manufacturer of targets for archery and rifle sport competitions. There are two parts to the analysis:

1) are the cash flows from the investment attractive enough? and

2) how should Archer raise a portion of the acquisition cost using debt?

Part 1:   The Investment

The projected cash flows from the Target Co. investment are shown below:

Year	Cash Flow
0	(500)
1	(100)
2	60
3	50
4	100
5	70
6	Cash flows for year 6 are 4.0% greater than for year 5. After year 6 the cash flows continue to grow at 4.0% forever.

The investment opportunity rate that Archer uses for investments like Target Co. is 12.50%.

Question 1:

Is the investment in Target Co. attractive at a 12.50% rate? Calculate the Net Present Value.

NPV = [   ]

Question 2:

Redo your calculations from Question 1 using a growth rate of 3.0% for year 6 and subsequent years, and an investment opportunity rate of 15.00%.

NPV = [   ]

Answers are at the bottom of the page following the Underwriting

The Underwriting - continued

Next, suppose that the revised cash flows look like the following if Target Co. is sold at the end of year 4.

Year	Cash Flow
0	(500)
1	80
2	30
3	50
4	1,000

Question 3:

What is the internal rate of return of the cash flows? What is the modified internal rate of return using a reinvestment rate of 10.00%?

IRR =

MIRR =

Part II: The Debt Portion of the Financing

Archer has the following choices for the debt portion of the financing.

Eurobond:

A $250 million par value, 7.875% coupon bond (paid annually) with a ten-year maturity, priced at 101 with 2.00% fee, and other costs of $250,000.

Domestic Corporate:

A $250 million, 7.50% coupon bond (paid semi-annually) with a ten-year maturity, priced at 98 with a 0.75% fee, and other costs of $200,000.

Question 4:

What are the All-In-Costs of the two bond issues? Express your answers as both annual (effective) rates, and semi-annual (nominal) rates.

Effective rate AIC

Eurobond =

Corporate =

Semi-annual rate AIC

Eurobond =

Corporate =

Part I

1. NPV = 70.190

2. NPV = (118.014)

3. IRR = 26.279%

 MIRR = 24.409%

Part II

4. Eurobond AIC = 8.039% effective, 7.884% SA

 Corporate AIC = 8.072% effective, 7.915% SA

5. $9,838,888.89

Answers to The Underwriting

The Underwriting - continued

Question 5:

Suppose instead of the two bond alternatives above, that Archer was able to borrow $500 million from their bank at 7.70%. Bank interest is calculated on a money market (simple interest) actual/360 basis. How much interest would Archer owe at the end of the first three months if the period has 92 days in it?

Interest = ⬚

APPENDIX 1: USING YOUR CALCULATOR

The HP-12C calculator provides a powerful resource for aiding in the speedy solution of financial math problems. Let's get to know them. For a more thorough coverage of their specific functions take a look at your *HP-12C Owner's Handbook and Problem-Solving Guide.*

Let's get started

Turn your calculator on by pressing the ON button on the lower left hand side of the keyboard. The display indicates that the calculator is ready to perform.

THE MAIN MENU

Reverse Polish Notation—RPN

The HP-12C is designed to use an arithmetic method called **Reverse Polish Notation** or RPN. The term honors Jan Llukasiewicz, a famous Polish mathematician who invented the method. You'll find the keyboard distinctive: it has no equal sign and no parentheses. Do ordinary arithmetic operations by inputting the first number, pressing ENTER to indicate that the first number is complete, inputting the second number, and then pressing the binary operator you wish to use (+, –, x or divide). Here is an example adding 6 to 9 to get 15.

6 ENTER
9 +
Result: 15.

RPN is fast and once you get used to it, easier to use than ordinary algebraic (left to right) arithmetic. Later versions of HP calculators, the 17B and 19B, have a switch in the MODES menu that allows the user to choose either RPN or ALG arithmetic. The HP-12C, however, has only one mode, RPN.

You can chain several operations together in RPN. Note the following.
6 ENTER 9 ENTER 5 ENTER 3 + + + result 23.

While it waits for you to input the binary operator, the calculator stores inputs in the Stack, an important feature of RPN. More on the Stack and multiple operations can be found in the HP Owners Guide in Appendix A. It is worth studying and will make you much more efficient with the calculator.

Shift Keys

To save room on the keyboard, the calculator has several multifunction keys. Note that each key has a white operation indicated directly on top of the key and may have a blue function on the lower face. Some may even have a gold function shown above the key. To access the blue or gold functions you must press the blue (g) or gold (f) shift key just prior to pressing the function key.

For instance the key will raise a value, y, to the x power if you choose the white function. The same key will calculate the square root of a value, x, if you choose the blue (g) function, or it will calculate the price of a US Treasury bond or note if you choose the gold (f) function.

Setting the Displayed Precision to the Right of the Decimal Point

To set the number of decimal places displayed, press f then number. If you wish to show five places to the right of the decimal, press

f 5.

The calculator actually keeps ten places of accuracy internally. You are affecting only how many places are displayed. It will round the number that is displayed, but not the actual number itself.

Using and clearing registers

The HP-12C has a number of registers used for calculations and information storage. The display is called the x register and several of the key functions use the

letter x to describe what they do. For instance the key's blue function is the square root of x, i.e., the square root of whatever is in the display. The working registers in the Stack are the x, y, z and t registers.

In addition to these registers there are twenty that you can use to store information you for later use. Use the STO key to store values. To store the number 214.5 in storage register 9 type

214.5 **STO** 9.

Later when you want to retrieve the value from register 9 recall it by pressing

RCL 9 result 214.5.

Access the first ten registers by pressing **STO number**, where number is the number of the storage register, 0, …, 9. Access the remaining ten by typing a decimal point just before the number of the register. For instance 214.5   STO   .8 will store the value 214.5 in storage register ".8" from where it can be recalled later.

To clear the display, press the CLx key. To clear all the registers, including the storage registers you have used, press f CLEAR REG. This action sets all the values in the registers to zero. As you can see from the keyboard, you can be more selective about which of the registers you clear (such as clearing only the FIN registers.)

Make it a habit to clear all registers before starting a new calculation. You don't want old stored numbers creeping into your calculations.

Time Value of Money (TVM)

The TVM keys deal with problems involving a single cash flow (FV or PV), a series of even cash flows called an annuity (PMTs), or a combination of PMTs, PV and FV. Sometimes we will want to calculate one of the values, and at other times we will want to calculate an interest rate, i, based on those values. These are in white on the top row left of the calculator.

Cash Flow

Cash Flow keys deal with problems in which there are several cash flows that cannot be fit into the PV, FV, and PMTs format of the TVM keys. This occurs where there are *uneven* cash flows. The cash flow keys are in blue on the second row center left of the calculator.

Using the TVM menu

On the top row left side of the calculator are:

The designers at Hewlett Packard set these keys up for use with specific problems in which the initial cash flow is negative, followed by positive cash flows later; or loans in which there is a positive cash flow followed by repayments (negative cash flows).

If you forget to follow this convention and put in all your entries as positive numbers when you are trying to calculate an interest rate, you will get the error message

Error 5

Here is how you might use the TVM keys.

Warning

EXAMPLE

You invested $1,000 at 6.00% for 5 years. You want to know how much you will have at the end of the fifth year. In the view of the calculator there is a cash outflow (the investment) at time 0 and a positive value at time 5 which we will now calculate.

The calculator entries are

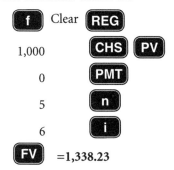

=1,338.23

The fourth step is a cautionary one to ensure that there is no value remaining in the PMT register left over from some prior calculation.

It was not really necessary in this case since you started the key sequence with

You will be surprised how often these old values can jump out and bite you when you least expect it, so get in the habit of zeroing out the unused registers when you do a calculation. Note that it does not matter which order you press the first four keys. However, you must press the FV key last, since that is the value you want.

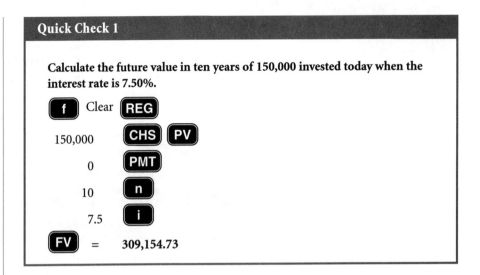

Quick Check 1

Calculate the future value in ten years of 150,000 invested today when the interest rate is 7.50%.

Do
the quick checks
to make sure you
understand

Bull

*An optimistic
investor who thinks
prices will rise*

Next suppose you know the present value and future value and want the interest rate or yield. Suppose that the present value is (1,000) and that the future value in ten years is 2,350. The keystrokes for the yield are:

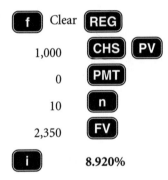

Quick Check 2

What is the yield on an investment that costs 750,000 today and will pay 1,250,000 in eight years?

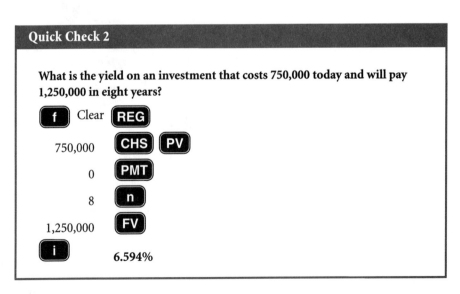

To calculate the present value today of 1,000 to be received in 5 years when the appropriate interest rate is 9.45%, the steps are as follows:

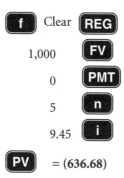

Cook the books

When a company's financial statements are intentionally falsified

You would interpret this to say, "In order to have 1,000 at the end of five years when the interest rate is 9.45%, you need to invest 636.68 today."

Quick Check 3

What is the present value at 9.52% of a cash flow of 100,000 to be received in 15 years?

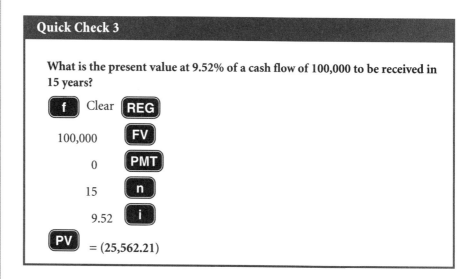

Next look at the PMT key. Suppose that you want to buy an apartment and plan to borrow $100,000 to finance a portion of the purchase price. You will use a residential mortgage loan at an interest rate of 6.00%, to be repaid with equal annual payments over fifteen years. In this case you want to calculate the annual payment (PMT) due on your loan. The key strokes are:

f	Clear REG
0	FV
100,000	PV
15	n
6.00	i
PMT	= (10,296.28)

Quick Check 4

Suppose you borrow 100,000 at a rate of 0.5% per month (this is usually referred to as 6% per year with monthly compounding) and make level monthly repayments for 120 months. What will your monthly payments be?

	f	Clear	REG
	0		FV
	100,000		PV
	120		n
	0.5		i
PMT		= (1,110.21)	

Your monthly payment will be 1,110.21.

Alternatively, suppose that you want to buy a ten-year annuity of payments of 10,000 when interest rates for such financial instruments is 8.44%. What will you have to pay to buy the right to receive these payments? The key strokes are:

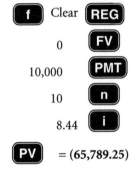

	f	Clear	REG
	0		FV
	10,000		PMT
	10		n
	8.44		i
PV		= (65,789.25)	

Bullet bonds and the calculator

Finally, let's consider the case of a "bullet" bond in which there are annual coupon interest payments (PMTs), a final payment of the face value or par value (FV) at maturity (n), and a market yield (i). More specifically suppose that the par value is 100, the coupon interest payments are 6.50 each, the maturity is ten years, and the market yield is 7.55%.

Use the PMT key for coupon payments on the calculator

The key strokes to calculate the price on a payment date are:

f	Clear	**REG**
100		**FV**
6.50		**PMT**
10		**n**
7.55		**i**
PV	= (92.81)	

Alternatively, we can calculate the yield for the same bond if we are given the price. Suppose that the price is 98.

98	**CHS**	**PV**
i	6.782%	

The yield is 6.782% when the price is 98. Notice that since the calculator remembers the values for the other parts of the bond, we did not have to reenter them. All we had to do was change the price (PV).

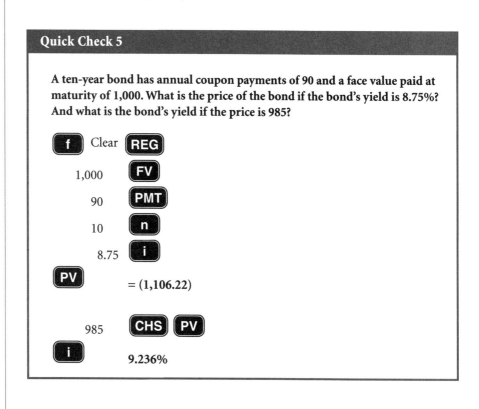

Quick Check 5

A ten-year bond has annual coupon payments of 90 and a face value paid at maturity of 1,000. What is the price of the bond if the bond's yield is 8.75%? And what is the bond's yield if the price is 985?

f	Clear	**REG**
1,000		**FV**
90		**PMT**
10		**n**
8.75		**i**
PV	= (1,106.22)	
985	**CHS**	**PV**
i	9.236%	

Using the Cash Flow Keys

The cash flow keys are in blue on the top row at the left center of the calculator. You must press **g shift** before you use the cash flow keys. When you use the cash flow keys, the calculator expects to solve a problem in which there is a cash flow at time zero, called CF_0. The cash flow can be either positive or negative.

Then the calculator expects a cash flow at every successive time point of the time period covered by the problem. You must enter these cash flows in the order they occur in the problem.

You can enter duplicate cash flows individually, or you can use the Nj key to indicate the number of identical cash flows. The cash flow itself called CFj is a distinct cash flow, i.e., different from the cash flow before it or after it.

Here is an example of how to enter the cash flows for a simple problem.

Time	Cash Flow	To input these press		
		f	CLEAR	REG
0	(100)	100	CHS	g CF0
1	50	50 →	g CF$_j$	2g N$_j$
2	50			
3	75	75 →	g CF$_j$	3g N$_j$
4	75			
5	75			
6	100	100	g CF$_j$	

To calculate the NPV at 10% press 10 **i** **f** **NPV** result 197.37. To calculate the IRR press **f** **IRR** result 56.04%.

Note that there are three distinct cash flows after CF_0. They are 50, 75 and 100. Press RCL n to see the number 3 which is the number of distinct cash flows if you are curious.

Quick Check 6

Calculate the net present value at 12% and the internal rate of return for the following set of cash flows.

Time	Cash Flow
0	(500)
1	80
2	400
3	200

Press the following keys:

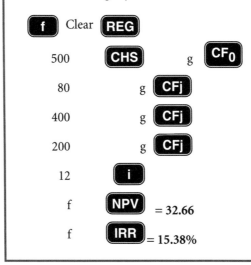

f	Clear **REG**
500	**CHS** g **CF₀**
80	g **CFj**
400	g **CFj**
200	g **CFj**
12	**i**
f	**NPV** = 32.66
f	**IRR** = 15.38%

Poison pill

A defense tactic by a target company to help prevent being taken over. It usually involves the existing shareholders being able to buy additional shares at a bargain price.

OTHER FEATURES OF THE HP-12C

Periods Less Than One Year

The HP-12C normally calculates simple interest for any value of n less than one. If you calculate the future value of 100.00 in 0.5 periods at an interest rate of 10% you will get 105.00 which is the simple interest calculation.

$$FV = PV * [1 + n*i]$$

In this case

$$105 = 100 * [1 + 0.5*0.10]$$

This feature also applies for periods greater than one. If you use a value of n of 2.5 periods, the result will be 127.05

$$127.05 = 100 * [1 + 0.10]^2 * [1 + 0.5*0.10]$$

This is a nice feature for money market applications or when calculating accrued interest on bonds. It allows you to use the TVM keys and have them use simple interest rather than compound interest (for the fractional part of n).

Sometimes you do not want simple interest calculations for fractional values of n. In such cases you can change the mode of operation of the calculator from simple to compound interest by giving it a special signal. The signal is to press STO EEX. When you do so a small letter "c" will appear on the lower right of the display to warn you that the calculator is in compound interest mode. To return the mode to simple interest press STO EEX again.

Weighted Averages

Occasionally you will want to calculate a weighted average of several values. The weighted average expression is

$$X_W = W_1{}^*V_1 + W_2{}^*V_2 + W_3{}^*V_3 + \ldots + W_N{}^*V_N$$

The W_i are the weights and the V_i are the values for which the weighted average is to be calculated. Normally, the sum of the weights is equal to one.

The HP-12C does the calculation quite efficiently. You won't need to normalize the weights so that they sum to one. Here is an example.

Values	Weights
146	25
178	18
200	10
250	5

To calculate the weighted average press the following keys.

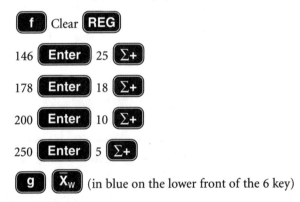

result = 174.2.

Raising a number to a power

To raise 1.05 to the tenth power, you can press the following keys:

1.05 **Enter**   10 **yˣ**

CHECKING OUT AND RESETTING THE CALCULATOR

To check the calculator, use its internal diagnostic capability. Do the following.

Turn the calculator OFF. Press the **ON** key and hold it down. Press the **X** (multiply) key and hold it down. Release the **ON** key. Release the X key. The calculator should flash the word 'running.' In a few seconds if everything is OK it will display the following.

-8,8,8,8,8,8,8,8,8,8,

USER f g BEGIN GRAD D.MY C PRGM

Relax—your calculator is working fine.

Resetting the Calculator

On rare occasions, the calculator will seem to malfunction on certain calculations. We don't know exactly how it gets into this state, but resetting it to its factory default settings usually fixes the problem. The keystrokes are similar to the diagnostic above.

> Turn the calculator OFF.
> Press **ON** and hold it down.
> Press **–** (the minus sign) and hold it down.
> Release the **ON** key.
> Release the **–** sign. The display should show **Pr Error.**

Press any key. The display should show two places to the right of the decimal point (the factory setting) and all registers should be set to zero. The internal switches should all be reset as well and you should be able to proceed without any problem.

That's it!

Well, that is it for our review of the calculator. To learn more, and there is more to learn, refer to the Owner's Manual. Many people find that at this point it is a good idea to work with the calculator on a few financial math problems for a while, and return to more detailed descriptions of the calculators operations later.

APPENDIX 2: ALGEBRA BRUSH-UP

Financial math can involve long and complex equations. Algebra uses symbols to represent different variables in equations.

So instead of saying:

"The interest amount is equal to the principal amount multiplied by the relevant interest rate,"

you can show this as an equation using words:

Interest = Principal * Interest Rate,

or reduce it still further by using symbols:

Interest

$$I = P * i$$

I	=	Interest amount
P	=	Principal
i	=	interest rate per period

You can use different amounts for P and i as the problem requires, but the relationship is constant.

In much of financial math, the underlying equation you will use is:

Future Value

$$FV = PV * (1 + i)^n$$

FV	=	Future Value of an investment
PV	=	Present Value of an investment
i	=	Interest rate per period
n	=	Number of periods

The purpose of the algebra review is to help you to brush up on using symbols in equations and show you how to manipulate them.

Using Symbols in Equations

In financial math, symbols represent quantities. For instance, PV might represent the amount you want to invest today. Or it might refer to the amount that you need to invest to have enough money for college tuition eighteen years from now. In an equation, individual symbols are called **variables.**

Usually mathematicians select symbols that are mnemonic, i.e. so that they remind them of what they are representing. You could rewrite the previous equation as:

$$KGH! = aJXX * (1 + DDL)^{yz}$$

The structure is the same, but the selection of symbols is terrible! You could never remember what they all meant and it would slow you down to a crawl.

Balloon payment

A loan or mortgage in which repayments are made in large chunks, or "balloons"

Symbols in Financial Math

Financial math is disciplined about variable names and chooses names that are easy to figure out at first sight. Here are a few:

Rates of interest or return or yield:	i, r, y, YTM
Initial investments or present values:	PV, I_0 , CF_0 (cash flows)
Single future payments:	FV, CFj
Time:	n, t
Counting indexes:	j, k, l, m

Operators and Expressions

Symbols by themselves are pretty meaningless until we use operators to explain their relationship to one another. Common operators include, addition "+", subtraction "−", multiplication "*", division "÷" or "/", and power "^" or "y^x".

Equations are split up into **expressions.** These are collections of symbols and operators.

The Equal Sign

There is usually an equal sign separating two expressions:

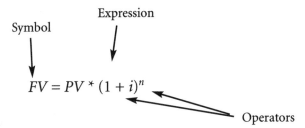

The equal sign tells us the value on both sides of the equation is the same. Usually the equation is set up in such a way that the symbol you want to calculate is on the left of the equal sign all by itself and all the other variables, whose values you know, are on the right hand side of the equal sign.

The equation above is set up to calculate the value of the future value when you know the values of PV, i and n. In other problems you may want to calculate the present value, PV, or perhaps the interest rate, i.

Order of Operations

Operations, including +, −, *, ÷ (or /), y^x (or y^x in Excel or Lotus 123) are fairly obvious except for the order they are performed. The convention in mathematics is to perform the most powerful operation first, the next most powerful next, and the least powerful last. Follow this Order:

1. **Exponentiation or raising to a power.**
2. **Multiplication and division.**
3. **Addition and subtraction.**

Exponentiation is symbolized by Y^X, in some calculators, and $Y^\wedge X$ in Excel, Lotus 123 and other calculators. Use the Y^X form here. Follow the next equation:

$$5 + 4 * 3^2 = 41$$

First raise the 3 to the 2nd power (3 * 3) to get 9.

Then multiply 9 by 4 to get 36.

And finally add 5 to 36 to obtain 41.

Notice how the discussion of the above calculation is much longer than the equation itself.

EXERCISE 45 ➤
Solve Them

Solve Them!

Solve the following equations

1. $2^3 * 3^2 + 4^2 =$

2. $9 * 3 + 2^5 =$

3. $22 + 3^2 * 3 =$

4. $2^3 * 3^2 * 4^2 =$

5. $4 + 16 + 3^3 * 4 =$

6. $5 + 4 * 3^2 =$

Parentheses and the Order of Operations

When you want the order to be different from the normal convention, put operations to be calculated first in parentheses (also known as brackets). Always calculate operations within parentheses first.

$$24 * (45 + 54) * 8^3$$

First, add 45 and 54 to give:

$$24 * 99 * 8^3$$

You can now solve the equation by taking 8 to the third power giving 512 and multiplying it by 99 to give 50,688, and finally multiplying by 24 to give 1,216,512.

EXERCISE 46 ➤
Symbols in Equations

Symbols in Equations

For the following questions $a = 5$, $b = 4$, $c = 3$, and $d = 2$. Substitute the numbers for the symbols and solve the equations:

1. $a + b * c^d =$

2. $(a + b) * c^d =$

3. $a + (b * c)^d =$

4. $[a + (b * c)]^d =$

Baby bond

A bond with a par value of less than $1,000

WHY EXPONENTS?

Exponents are intended to simplify expressions that otherwise might get pretty large. They are particularly useful in financial math as the next case demonstrates:

Suppose you deposit some money in your savings account at the local bank. Assign your deposit the symbol "PV". The interest rate you earn on your money per year will be "i". Assume interest is paid once a year at the end of the year.

At the end of one year you will have your investment, PV, plus what you have earned during the year in interest i * PV. At the end of the year you can calculate your future value using the following equation:

$$FV = PV + P * i$$

Rewrite:

$$FV = PV * (1 + i)$$

where the 1 in the parentheses refers to the repayment of your original deposit (also known as the principal) at the end of the investment, and the i refers to the interest. In other words *PV* is equal to *PV * 1*.

Interest on Interest

Now consider what happens if you do this for a second year at the same interest rate, i. You will have

$$FV \text{ (at the end of two years)} = PV * (1 + i) * (1 + i)$$

Normally, algebraic convention says you should leave out the multiplication sign writing simply:

$$FV \text{ (at the end of two years)} = PV * (1 + i)(1 + i)$$

You have just learned the equation used for **compounding,** where the future value of an investment is made up of the principal repayment, the two interest payments and the interest on the first interest payment. Interest on interest is called **compound interest.** You'll find out more about compounding in the main part of the book.

Here is where the use of exponents helps. Start with a quantity, *a*, called the base. Then:

$$a = a^1,$$

$$a * a = a^2,$$

$$a * a * a = a^3,$$

$$\underbrace{a * a * a * \ldots * a}_{n} = a^n.$$

Notice how much more compact exponential notation is. Textbook editors who want to save space would have invented it if mathematicians had not invented it first.

From the previous example you can rewrite:

$$FV \text{ (at the end of two years)} = PV * (1 + i)(1 + i)$$

as

$$FV \text{ (after two periods)} = PV * (1 + i)^2,$$

and more generally,

$$FV \text{ (after n periods)} = PV * (1 + i)^n$$

Here the n tells you how many time periods separate an investment's future value from its present value.

EXERCISE 47 ➤
Expotential!

Expotential!

1. Calculate $a * a * a * a =$
   when $a = 1.10$.

   [   ]

2. Calculate $c * c * c * c * c =$
   when $c = 1.05$

   [   ]

3. Calculate $\dfrac{1}{d*d*d}$ when $d = 1.10$.

4. Calculate $\dfrac{d*d}{e*e*e}$ when $d = 2$ and $e = 3$.

5. Calculate $\left(\dfrac{1+g}{1+i}\right) * \left(\dfrac{1+g}{1+i}\right) * \left(\dfrac{1+g}{1+i}\right)$

   when $g = 0.05$, and $i = 0.09$.

Use the calculator to solve this problem

It is easy to raise a number to a power using your calculator. For example, to raise 2.65 to the fourth power:

2.65 **Enter**   4   **yˣ**   = 49.316

RULES OF EXPONENTS

Rule 1: Multiplying Expressions with Exponents

If you want to multiply two expressions with the same base then just add the exponents:

$$a^n * a^m = a^{n+m}$$

The rule of multiplying exponents is useful when you want to compound your investment further into the future. For example, if instead of compounding out two years you wanted to compound an investment out a further three years you could simply add the two exponents:

$$(1 + 0.10)^2 * (1 + 0.10)^3 = (1 + 0.10)^5.$$

If the bases are not the same there is no way to combine them nicely, so you must calculate the values separately.

EXERCISE 48 ➤
Simplify Me

Simplify Me

1. Simplify the following expression and evaluate it when $x = 2$.

   $$x^3 * x^4 = \boxed{}$$

2. Simplify and evaluate the following equation when $d = 1.045$.

   $$d^4 * d^2 = \boxed{}$$

3. Simplify and evaluate the following equation when $f = 0.01$.

   $$(1 + f)^3 * (1 + f)^{10} \boxed{}$$

Rule 2: Raising an Expression with an Exponent to a Power

If you have an expression with an exponent and you want to raise it to a power the rule is:

$$(a^n)^m = a^{n*m}$$

Calculate . . .

1. Simplify.

$$\left(a^3\right)^2 =$$

2. Calculate.

$$\left(1.10^6\right)^2 =$$

3. Simplify and evaluate the following equation when $f = 0.05$.

$$\left[\left(1 + f\right)^2\right]^5 =$$

Rule 3: Negative Exponents

A negative exponent is equal to 1 divided by the positive exponent:

$$a^{-n} = \frac{1}{a^n}$$

One divided by a number is called the **"reciprocal"** of the number.

Here is an example of a negative exponent used in financial math:

$$\left(1 + 0.10\right)^{-5} = \frac{1}{\left(1 + 0.10\right)^5}$$

The formula below shows a negative exponent being used to **discount** a value back from five periods in the future to the present. The general equation is:

$$PV = FV * \left(1 + 0.10\right)^{-n}$$

In other words, an investment's present value is equal to its future value multiplied by 1 plus the interest rate taken to the negative number of periods exponent.

Simplify and Evaluate

1. Simplify and evaluate when $a = 2$.

$$a^5 * a^6 =$$

2. Simplify and evaluate when $a = 1.05$.

$$a^{-5} * a^2 =$$

3. Simplify and evaluate the following equation when $f = 0.01$.

$$(1 + f)^{-3} * (1 + f)^2 * (1 + f)^{-1} =$$

Rule 4: Fractional Exponents

Fractional exponents refer to roots of a number. For example

$$\sqrt{x} = x^{1/2}.$$

When you multiply two similar expressions with fractional exponents, you simply add the two fractions. For instance

$$x^{1/2} * x^{1/2} = x^1 = x, \text{ and}$$
$$\sqrt{x} * \sqrt{x} = x.$$

EXERCISE 51 ➤
More Simplify and Evaluate

More Simplify and Evaluate

1. Simplify and evaluate when $x = 16$.

   $x^{\frac{1}{2}} =$ ☐

2. Calculate the following when $x = 3$.

   $x^{\frac{1}{2}} * x^{\frac{1}{2}} =$ ☐

3. Calculate and evaluate the following when $x = 1.09$

   $x^{\frac{1}{3}} * x^{\frac{1}{4}} =$ ☐

Solving Equations

Financial math frequently requires you to solve equations. You have to manipulate the equation (without breaking the relationship described by the equal sign) to isolate one symbol on one side of the equal sign leaving all the other symbols on the other side of the equal sign. When an equation has only one symbol on one side, and none of the same symbols are on the other side, it's in "closed form."

Rules for Solving Equations:

The rules we apply to an equation are as follows:

1. **Multiply or divide both sides of the equation by the same amount.**
2. **Add or subtract the same value to both sides of the equal sign.**
3. **Raise both sides of an equation to the same power or root.**

These rules can be applied several times and in any order.

EXAMPLE

Solve for x in the equation

$$4x + 1 = 3y + x + 7$$

Step 1

Subtract 1 from both sides resulting in

$$4x = 3y + x + 6$$

Step 2

Subtract x from both sides resulting in

$$3x = 3y + 6$$

Step 3

Divide both sides by 3 resulting in

$$x = y + 2$$

At this point the equation cannot be reduced further. It says that the value of x is always going to be 2 more than the value of y.

The value of x is not known absolutely but is dependent on the value of y. This is called a **conditional relationship.** If y were equal to 6, x would be 8, and so on.

EXERCISE 52 ➤
Solve Them

Solve Them

1. Solve the following for z.
   $6z + 9 = 4z + 26$

2. Solve the following for w.
   $2(6w + 3y) = 10w + 16$

3. Solve the following for x.
   $3x + 3y = y^2 - x$

Distributing

Two very common operations you will encounter involve distributing and factoring of expressions. They are the reverse of each other. Here's an example of distributing:

$$2(x + y) = 2x + 2y$$

In the above case the 2 is distributed across the $(x + y)$.

$$x^2y(2 + 3z) = 2x^2y + 3x^2yz$$

In the above example the distribution is done term by term. First the multiplier x^2y is multiplied by the 2. Then the x^2y is multiplied by the 3z.

EXERCISE 53 ➤
Distribute!

Distribute!

Distribute the multiplier in the problems below:

1. $13(x + 3y) =$

2. $x(x + 3y + z) =$

3. $(x + y) * (2 + 3z) =$

Factoring

The reverse of distributing is factoring. Example;

$$2a + 2b = 2(a + b).$$

Here the 2 is a common factor of both terms on the left hand side of the equal sign. Another example is:

$$3x^2 y + 6xz = 3x(xy + 2z)$$

EXERCISE 54 ➤
Factor!

Factor!

Factor the following equations:

1. $20a + 40b =$

2. $2x^2y + 8xy =$

3. $1/2\ cd + 1/2\ ck + c =$

SOLVING FINANCIAL MATH EQUATIONS

To find compound interest (where you earn interest on interest that you have already earned), calculate future value using the following equation:

$$FV = PV * (1 + i)^n$$

Using your knowledge of solving equations you can determine the equation which will solve for present value. Divide both sides by $(1 + i)^n$, resulting in:

$$\frac{FV}{(1 + i)^n} = PV$$

or write it as

$$PV = FV * (1 + i)^{-n}$$

EXERCISE 55 ➤
Solve, Solve, Solve . . .

Solve, Solve, Solve . . .

1. Solve the following equation for k.

$$PV = \frac{CF_1}{k - g}$$

2. Solve for x when $y = 3$.

$$x + y^2 + xy = 16$$

3. Solve for p in the following when $k = 2$.

$$4p + pk + 3 = 30 - 2pk$$

SIGMA NOTATION

Many Time Value of Money problems have several cash flows. A thirty-year home mortgage with monthly payments has the initial mortgage loan plus 360 monthly payments. It's cumbersome to write down algebraic expressions including each individual mortgage payment. A much simpler format for these equations uses **Sigma** or **Summation** notation.

EXAMPLE

Suppose you wanted to know the average age of a group of people. You would add, or sum, the ages of each of the people, and divide by the number of people in the group.

Suppose there were five people, whose ages were 17, 25, 18, 23, 27. Your equation to calculate their average age would be:

$$\text{Average} = \frac{17 + 25 + 18 + 23 + 27}{5} = 22$$

The individual items of data are called **observations.**

If there were 50 people our equation would be unbearably large. Here is a summation shortcut. Label each of the observations something like A_1, A_2, A_3, A_4, and A_5, where the numbers 1, 2, . . . 5 are referred to as the **index.** You can generalize your notation and show an observation as Aj, where j can take on any value from 1 through 5 in this case.

So far you have:

$$\text{Average} = \frac{A_1 + A_2 + A_3 + A_4 + A_5}{5}$$

Where $A_1 = 17$, $A_2 = 25$ etc.

Next simplify the expression using the capital Greek letter sigma (for sum) S:

$$\sum_{j=1}^{j=5} A_j = A_1 + A_2 + A_3 + A_4 + A_5$$

Above the sigma letter is the total number of observations, underneath is the point where you start adding the observations.

Next,

$$\frac{\sum_{j=1}^{j=5} x_i}{5} = \text{Average}$$

More generally the equation is written as:

$$\frac{\sum_{j=1}^{j=n} x_i}{n} = \text{Average of } n \text{ observations}$$

EXAMPLE - continued

Note that if you have 800 observations the equation does not get any more complicated:

$$\frac{\sum_{j=1}^{j=800} x_i}{800} = \text{Average of 800 observations}$$

EXERCISE 56 ➤
Sigma

Sigma

1. You have six items $a_1 = 3$, $a_2 = 4$, $a_3 = 7$, $a_4 = 10$, $a_5 = 2$, and $a_6 = 6$. Calculate the following equation:

$$\frac{\sum_{k=1}^{k=6} a_k}{3}$$

2. Calculate the following where $CF_1 = 100$, $CF_2 = 50$, and $f = 1.10$.

$$\sum_{j=1}^{j=2} \frac{CF_j}{f^j}$$

3. Calculate the following when $x_1 = 6$, $x_2 = 9$, $x_3 = 16$, and $x_4 = 22$.

$$\frac{\sum_{j=1}^{j=4} x_j}{4}$$

Sigma Notation and Time Value of Money

Use summation or sigma notation in Time Value of Money problems wherever you have a series of cash flows. Here is an example:

Killer bees

Investment bankers who help a company fight off a takeover bid

EXAMPLE

Suppose you are evaluating an investment opportunity which generates the following cash flows:

Time	Cash Flow
1	100
2	300
3	200

You want to find the present value using an interest rate of 10%. Writing this out the long way you would have the following equation:

$$PV = \frac{100}{(1 + 0.1)^1} + \frac{300}{(1 + 0.1)^2} + \frac{200}{(1 + 0.1)^3}$$

EXAMPLE - continued

You could use sigma notation shortening it to:

$$PV = \sum_{j=1}^{j=3} \frac{CF_j}{(1+i)^j}$$

Where: j = 1,...,3

i = 0.1

CF_1 = 100

CF_2 = 300

CF_3 = 200

EXERCISE 57 ➤
Calculate the Value

Calculate the Value

1. Calculate the value below when $CF_0 = 100$, $i = 0.10$, and $g = 0.04$.

$$\sum_{k=1}^{k=3} \frac{CF_0(1+g)^k}{(1+i)^k}$$

2. Here are some more cash flows you are evaluating as an investment opportunity:

Time	Cash Flow
1	8
2	108

Calculate the value of D in the following equation:

$$D = \frac{\displaystyle\sum_{t=1}^{t=2} \frac{t * CF_t}{(1+y)^t}}{\displaystyle\sum_{t=1}^{t=2} \frac{CF_t}{(1+y)^t}}$$

Assume that y = 0.08 or 8.00%

Hit the phones

Hit the Phones! Summary

1. Algebra usually uses symbols to represent quantities in relationships. It helps a lot if the symbols are chosen to be mnemonic:

$$FV = PV * (1 + i)^n$$

These symbols should make you think of future value, present value etc.

2. Equations place expressions on both sides of an equal sign. You may start out with complicated-looking expressions, but you can simplify them. If you are interested in working out one variable, you "solve" the equation so that the variable you are interested in is on the left side of the equal sign all by itself.

3. The relationships of variables in expressions are shown with binary operations $(+, -, *, /$ or $\div,$ and y^x or $\wedge)$. Exponentiation goes first, multiplication and division second and addition and subtraction last. Parentheses are used to force a different sequence of operations.

4. Exponents follow simple rules:

$$a^n * a^m = a^{n+m}$$

$$\left(a^n\right)^m = a^{n*m}$$

$$a^{-n} = \frac{1}{a^n}$$

$$\sqrt{x} = x^{1/2}$$

$$a^{\frac{1}{r}} = r^{\text{th}} \text{ root of } a$$

5. Equations are solved (or simplified) by using rules that apply operations to both sides of an equation. You can add/subtract, multiply/divide or raise to a power, as long as you do so on both sides. A great deal of financial math involves manipulating equations using these techniques.

6. You can reduce the size of an equation by distributing a common variable across other variables. Reversing distribution is called factoring.

$$2(x + y) = 2x + 2y$$

7. If a number of items or terms are added (summed) we often use sigma notation to make the expressions more compact. For example:

$$\sum_{j=1}^{j=5} A_j = A_1 + A_2 + A_3 + A_4 + A_5$$

That's it for the algebra used in financial math. Try the due diligence questions as a final check.

Due Diligence

1. What would be good symbols to use for the following?

Weight

Height

Profit

Revenues

Free Cash Flow

2. Solve the following for CF and evaluate it when $i = 0.09$, and $PV = 100$.

$$PV = \frac{CF}{(1+i)^1} + \frac{CF}{(1+i)^2}$$

3. Calculate the value below when $i = 0.01$.

$$\left[(1+i)^{12}\right]^4$$

4. Calculate the following when $CF_1 = 50$, $CF_2 = 60$, and $CF_3 = 20$ and $i = 0.08$.

$$\sum_{j=1}^{j=3} \frac{CF_j}{(1+i)^j}$$

Factoring will help you here.

Answers to Due Diligence for Algebra Review

1. Weight — W

Height — h

Profit — P or Prof or π

Revenues — R or S (for sales)

Free Cash Flow — FCF

2. 56.847

3. 1.61223

4. 113.613

Exercise 1 - Saver or capital user?

1. Saver
2. Capital user
3. Saver
4. Capital user

Exercise 2 - Debt or Equity?

1. Equity
2. Aggressive
3. Equity holdings
4. Equity
5. Yes

Exercise 3 - Show me the money!

1. High yield loans
2. Senior debt will be repaid first and subordinate debt will be paid last.
3. A senior debt loan

Exercise 4 - Bonds

1. High yield bonds
2. Large companies with recognized names
3. Bonds are often a cheaper way for a company to raise money.
4. Pension funds, insurance companies and fund managers
5. Usually $1,000

Exercise 5 - The Equity Markets

1. Earnings per share
2. No
3. Share certificates
4. Rewards
5. In an IPO or initial public offering, a company issues shares on the stock exchange for the first time.

Exercise 6 - The Pitch

1. It is better to receive money earlier as you can invest it and generate a return.
2. You can invest money over time and generate a return.
3. Present value
4. It's better to have a higher interest rate. A higher interest rate means you are generating a greater return on your money.
5. It's looking for the Present Value.

Exercise 7 - The Mandate

1. As an interest rate: 25%
   As an absolute $ number: $100,000

2. Interest: $1,050
   Loan: $15,000
   Total Future Value $16,050

3. Deposit required: $12,264.15

4. Yes you will have £160,695,000. If you were to keep any excess you would have £695,000, a tidy sum for one year's work!

5. It's looking for the present value.

$$\frac{\$150,000}{(1 + 0.0873)} = \$137,956.41$$

Exercise 8 - The Pitch

1. Using algebra
   The generic formula
   $FV = PV * (1+ i)^n$, so
   $FV = 50,000 * (1 + 0.812)^{20} = 238,281.73$
   $FV = 50,000 * (1 + 0.825)^{20} = 244,077.70$

   Using The Time Value of Money (TVM) Keys

   f Clear **REG**

   50,000 **CHS** **PV**

   0 **PMT**

   20 **n**

   8.12 **i**

   FV = 238,281.73

   8.25 **i**

   FV = 244,077.70

   Notice you don't have to re-input all the information again to solve the second part of the question.

   The TVM keys assume that all problems involve either investments (where the Present Value is negative), or loans (where the Present Value is positive and the Future Value is negative). You must make either the Future Value or the Present Value negative. Otherwise when you are solving for an interest rate, you will get an "ERROR 5" message! Watch out. It's easy to make mistakes.

2. $PV = \dfrac{1,000,000}{(1 + 0.812)^{20}} = 209,835.64$

   $PV = \dfrac{1,000,000}{(1 + 0.825)^{20}} = 204,852.80$

Compound Interest - The Pitch - continued

HP-12C Using The Time Value of Money (TVM) Keys

f Clear **REG**

100,000 **FV**

0 **PMT**

20 **n**

8.12 **i**

PV = (209,835.64)

8.25 **i**

PV = (204,852.80)

Notice all the problems using the calculator keys have **f** Clear **REG** at the top. Making sure all your storage registers are cleared is very important. It is easy to get wrong answers by not starting from a clean slate. Get into the habit now!

3. You want to calculate the Future Value of $120,000 at 5.0% for 18 years. The amount is $288,794.31, enough to make new parents pause!

4. You want to calculate the Present Value of $288,794 in 18 years at 6.50%. The amount is $92,959.81. Again enough to make one pause.

5. You want to calculate the Present Value of €10,000,000 after 40 years at 4.50%. The amount is €1,719,287.01.

Exercise 9 - The Mandate

1. **[f]** Clear **[REG]**

   1,000,000,000 **[CHS]** **[PV]**

   0 **[PMT]**

   10 **[n]**

   6.04 **[i]**

   [FV] = **1,797,617,099.64**

2. **[f]** Clear **[REG]**

   150,000,000 **[FV]**

   0 **[PMT]**

   7 **[n]**

   5.85 **[i]**

   [PV] = **(100,752,358.80)**

3. **[f]** Clear **[REG]**

   200,000,000 **[CHS]** **[PV]**

   0 **[PMT]**

   10 **[n]**

   1,000,000,000 **[FV]**

   [i] = **17.462%**

4. €152,951.14

5. ¥852,826

6. 9.596%

7. CDN7,414,917.24

Exercise 10 - The Pitch

1. This is a Future Value problem, where

   $FV = \$5,327.26 * (1 + 0.065)^{10} = \$10,000.00$

   [f] Clear **[REG]**

   5,327.26 **[CHS]** **[PV]**

   0 **[PMT]**

   10 **[n]**

   6.5 **[i]**

   [FV] = **10,000.00**

   The bond is not a savings account. You can't "with-draw" the money you invested. However, you can sell the bond to someone else. We will cover this later.

2. $PV = \dfrac{50,000}{(1 + 0.0628)^{13}} = \$22,651.00$

   [f] Clear **[REG]**

   50,000 **[FV]**

   0 **[PMT]**

   13 **[n]**

   6.28 **[i]**

   [PV] = **(22,651.65)**

3. ¥86,177,179

4. $32,866.55

5. ¥9,178,123

A N S W E R S

Exercise 11 - The Mandate

1. $i = \left(\dfrac{100}{32}\right)^{\frac{1}{15}} - 1 = 0.07892$

f Clear **REG**
32 **CHS** **PV**
0 **PMT**
15 **n**
100 **FV**

i **7.892%**

2. 7.958%

3. **Part 1:**
Calculate the purchase price in the beginning:

$PV = \dfrac{1,000}{(1 + 0.0875)^{30}} = 80.740$

Part 2:
Calculate the sale price two years later:

$PV = \dfrac{1,000}{(1 + 0.09100)^{28}} = 87.278$

Part 3:
Calculate the yield over the two years you owned the bond:

$\left(\dfrac{87.278}{80.746}\right)^{\frac{1}{2}} - 1 = 0.03966$

You buy it for 80.746 and sell it for 87.278. Therefore your yield over the two years is 3.966% p.a. Note p.a. means per annum or annually.

4. A diagram really helps with these questions.

Sale Price

5 years

Purchase Price

Question 4 is difficult. There are three steps to getting the answer:

Exercise 11- The Mandate - continued

Step 1: Calculate your investment:

f Clear **REG**
100 **FV**
0 **PMT**
20 **n**
8.10 **i**

FV = **(21.061)**

Step 2: Calculate the value you must receive in five years in order to earn a 10% return.

f Clear **REG**
21.06 **CHS** **PV**
0 **PMT**
5 **n**
10 **i**

FV = **33.920**

Step 3: Calculate the yield for 15-year zero coupon bonds when the price is 33.920:

f Clear **REG**
33.920 **CHS** **PV**
0 **PMT**
15 **n**
100 **FV**

i = **7.474%**

5. **f** Clear **REG**
63 **CHS** **PV**
0 **PMT**
2 **n**
83 **FV**

i = **14.781%**

Exercise 12 - Commercial Banks

1. Short term assets and liabilities
2. The Glass-Steagall Act
3. An institution tries to match its short-term liabilities with its short-term assets and its long-term liabilities with its long-term assets.
4. If it had a view on the direction of interest rates
5. Borrowers and investors using the security markets to deposit or borrow money, rather than using a commercial bank as an intermediary. More generally, savers dealing directly with capital users rather than going through an intermediary, such as a bank or life insurance company.

Exercise 13 - Savings and Loan

1. It depends on their maturity.
2. Sharply rising interest rates
3. Credit Unions are usually connected with the employment of one institution and concentrate on making consumer loans.
4. The Federal Reserve

Exercise 14 - Insure It!

1. Safe
2. By investing premiums before claims and expenses are paid out
3. An agreement to make a fixed payment regularly over time
4. Property and casualty insurance and life insurance
5. Highly

Exercise 15 - The Big Kahuna!

1. Defined benefit plans and defined contribution plans
2. Equities
3. Defined contribution plans
4. Government or private (corporations and unions) entities
5. $84,000

Exercise 16 - Finance & Invest. Cos.

1. A finance company
2. Specialists
3. You can easily redeem shares in an open-ended mutual fund. You sell shares in a closed fund to another investor.
4. A company which raises money by issuing securities, then uses it to make loans to individuals and businesses.
5. Illiquid

Exercise 17 - Investment Banks

1. Sales and trading, advising on mergers and acquisitions and underwriting
2. Proprietary trading
3. Large companies wanting to raise money in the capital markets and large investors wanting to invest money in the capital markets

Exercise 18 - The Pitch

1. A diagram really helps with these questions.

f	Clear	**REG**
	0	**FV**
	1,000,000	**PMT**
	5	**n**
	4.03	**i**

   PV = (4,448,072.95)

2. CHF (39,073,844.23)
3. $182,315.16
4. 3.810%

Exercise 19 - The Mandate

1. $PV = \dfrac{\$6.95}{0.08220} = \$84.55$

2. $Yield = \dfrac{\$6.95}{\$62.50} = 0.1112$

3. $\dfrac{6.50}{0.0815} = 79.75$

4. $\dfrac{10{,}100}{98{,}000} = 0.10306$

Exercise 20 - The Pitch

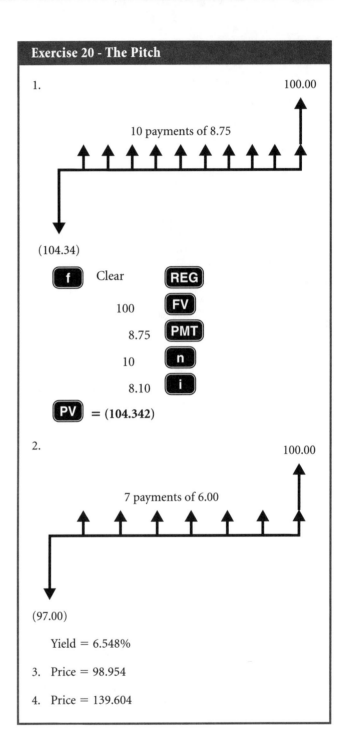

1.   100.00

10 payments of 8.75

(104.34)

f	Clear		REG
100		FV
8.75		PMT
10		n
8.10		i

PV = (104.342)

2.   100.00

7 payments of 6.00

(97.00)

Yield = 6.548%

3. Price = 98.954

4. Price = 139.604

Exercise 21 - The Mandate

1. Yield = 5.764%

2. Coupon = 7.894 remember, assume you are dealing with percentages.

3. Yield = 5.325%

4. Return = 19.669%. Remember to include the benefit of the coupon payment if you are using algebra to answer this problem. You invest 92 and one year later the bond is worth 102.595, plus you receive a coupon of 7.50. The increase from 92 to 110.095 is 19.669%.

5. You must have 121.165 at the end of one year. Of this 8.00 will come from the coupon, meaning that the rest must come from the selling price: 121.165 − 8.00 = 113.165. At that price with nine years remaining maturity and an 8.00% coupon, the yield must be 6.059%.

Exercise 22 - Developments in the Capital Markets

1. Lower funding costs for issuers

2. Shares in companies which are focused on one business, so investors can easily understand them

3. Modern communications and information systems have enabled investors and issuers to look for investing and funding opportunities on a worldwide basis

4. The performance of another asset

5. i. Selling and issuing securities has become cheaper.
   ii. The mutual fund business has become much larger and can support specialization.
   iii. The demise of the theory of diversification at the level of the company.

Exercise 23 - The Pitch

1. NPV (10.00%) = 10.07
   IRR = 16.346%

2. NPV (8.50%) = 8,683.78
   IRR = 27.808%

3. NPV (12.50%) = 581,588.17
   IRR = 23.597%

4. NPV (9.30%) = 158.97
   IRR = 16.448%

5. First calculate the NPV (10.00%) for cash flows 0, 1, and 2. Your answer so far should be 41.32. It is short of the goal of 150 by 108.68. We need 108.68 more Present Value, therefore we must make the terminal value high enough to have a PV of 108.68:

   Terminal Value = **$108.68 * 1.10^3 = 144.65$**

Exercise 24 - The Mandate

1. Future Value = 3,949.11

2. Change in Net Present Value
   NPV at 9.00%   961.10
   NPV at 9.01%   960.72
   Difference   (0.38)

3. Present Value = 473.00

4. Present Value = 969.32

5. Price you would pay = $2,345.74
   Gain = $345.74
   Note that $345.74 is the Net Present Value at 9.30% if the purchase price is $2,000

6. NPV(10%) = 35.289
   NPV(12%) = (35.897)
   You can guess the IRR is roughly between the two answers at 11%. The actual IRR = 10.966%.

Exercise 25 - The Pitch

1. **f** Clear **REG**

   0 g **CF₀**

   100 g **CFj**

   200 g **CFj**

   300 g **CFj**

   400 g **CFj**

   9 **i** **f** **NPV** = 775.10

   CHS **PV** 4 **n**

   FV = 1,094.12

2. **f** Clear **REG**

   0 g **CF₀**

   70 g **CFj** 5 g **Nj**

   90 g **CFj** 4 g **Nj**

   1,090 g **CFj**

   8 **i** **f** **NPV** = 987.25

   CHS **PV** 10 **n** **FV** 2,131.39

3. The calculation is easy to do using the Time Value of Money keys:

   f Clear **REG**

   0 **PV**

   80 **PMT**

   10 **n**

   7.55 **i**

   FV = 1,134.45

Exercise 26 - The Mandate

1. First calculate the Net Future Value at 10.50% of the cash flows at the end of periods 1, 2 and 3.

   Next use the TVM keys to calculate the MIRR at 10.50% = 11.781%.

2. Find the FV of the coupons at 7.25% = 46.236; add the final principal payment at maturity to get 146.513;

   Finally, use (103) for PV and solve for I%YR = 7.261%. So the RCY (7.55%) = 7.261%. Remember the RCY is the same as the MIRR.

3. For A, MIRR (8.50%) = 13.662%, for B, MIRR (8.50%) = 11.582%.

Exercise 27 - The Pitch

1. Cash Flow keys

1,000 **CFS** g **CF₀**

1,500 g **CFj**

0 g **CFj**

2 g **Nj**

530 **CFS** g **CFj**

0 **i** f **NPV** (30.00)

3 **i** f **NPV** (14.59)

6 **i** f **NPV** (4.72)

9 **i** f **NPV** 0.68

12 **i** f **NPV** 2.46

15 **i** f **NPV** 1.32

18 **i** f **NPV** (2.18)

2.

Interest rate	NPV
0%	(250.000)
3%	(115.957)
6%	(39.482)
9%	(2.098)
12%	8.794
15%	1.847
18%	(16.961)
21%	(43.486)

It looks like the IRRs are between 9% and 12% and between 15% and 18%.

Exercise 28 - The Mandate

1. X = 1, Y = 3, Z = 1.

2. IRRs = 8.584%, 27.672%.
   Make the investment if the return on your alternative investments is between 8.584% and 27.672%. Otherwise reject it.

3. There are three IRRs: 42.812%, 80.263%, and 224.424%.

4. Descartes' Rule of Signs says there may be as many as three solutions. In this case, however, there is only one, 18.439%.

5. There is only one solution = 6.999%.

Exercise 29 - The Pitch

1. Draw the diagram first:

   100
   −1
   = **99**

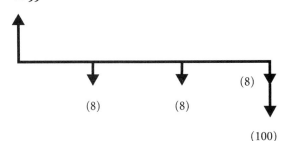

   All-In-Cost = 8.391%.

2. Draw the diagram first:

   99.5
   −1.5
   = **98.0**

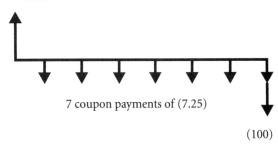

   7 coupon payments of (7.25)

   All-In-Cost = 7.629%.

Exercise 29 - The Pitch - continued

3. Draw the diagram first:

    100.5
    −0.65
    = **100.85**

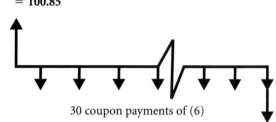

30 coupon payments of (6)

All-In-Cost = 5.939%.

4. The answer is easy. Since you are issuing at a premium that exactly equals the fee, you receive the par value when you issue. If the bond is issued at par (from your point of view), your AIC is equal to the coupon rate of 8.00%.

5. PV = 99.50 − 0.65 = 98.85

f	Clear	REG
	98.85	CHS PV
	06.25	CHS PMT
	3	n
	100	FV
i		= **6.686%**

Exercise 30 - The Mandate

1. Draw the diagram first:

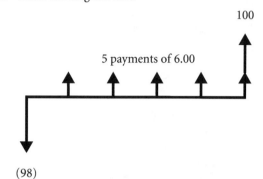

100

5 payments of 6.00

(98)

6.481%.

2. First, the other up-front costs are 0.10% (note "percent") of par. The cash flows are as follows:

    99.50
    −0.70
    −0.10
    = **98.70**

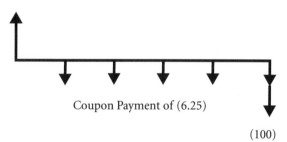

Coupon Payment of (6.25)

(100)

All-In-Cost = 6.563%.

3. The other up-front costs are 0.04% of par. Your cash flows are (expressed in percent of par) as follows:

    100.50
    −2.00
    −0.04
    = **98.46**

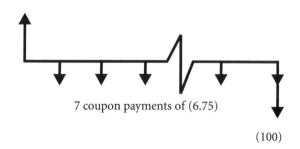

7 coupon payments of (6.75)

(100)

All-In-Cost = 7.036%.

Exercise 30 - The Mandate - continued

4. **Step 1:** Calculate the other costs as a percent of par

$$\frac{200,000}{500,000,000} * 100 = 0.04\%$$

Step 2: Calculate the AIC using the TVM keys:
$$PV = 101.5 - 2.00\ 0.04 = 99.46$$

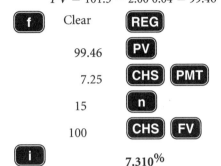

f	Clear	REG
99.46		PV
7.25		CHS PMT
15		n
100		CHS FV
i		**7.310%**

5. **Step 1:** Calculate other costs as a percent of par value
= 0.075%

Step 2: Calculate the AIC using the TVM keys:
$$PV = 100.500 - 1.875 - 0.075 = 98.550$$

f	Clear	REG
98.55		PV
6.375		CHS PMT
5		n
100		CHS FV
i		**6.726%**

Always check to capture errors. Being just a few decimal places out can spell disaster. Remember you are dealing with millions, possibly billions of dollars, or pounds or euros so a small error can translate into a significant number.

Exercise 31 - Interest Rates and Bond Yields

1. U.S. Treasury security yields

2. Relatively high risk

3. 8.08%

4. Standard and Poors, and Moody's Investor Services

5. Lower. A BBB rated bond is lower risk than a B rated bond.

Exercise 32 - The Pitch

1. $FV = 1,000,000 * \left(1 + \frac{0.06 * 90}{360}\right) = 1,015,000$

2. $FV = 50,000 * \left(\frac{0.0585 * 180}{360}\right) = 51,462.50$

3. $PV = 50,000 * \frac{10,000,000}{\left(1 + \frac{0.0497 * 270}{360}\right)} = 9,640,644.96$

4. $FV = 10,000,000 * \left(1 + \frac{0.0583 * 270}{360}\right) = 10,437,250.00$

5. $FV = 100,000,000 * \left(1 + \frac{0.0615 * 90}{360}\right) = 101,537,500$

Exercise 33 - The Mandate

1.
$$Interest = 250,000,000 * \left(\frac{0.0613 * 92}{360} \right) = 3,916,388.89$$

2.
$$FV = €1,000,000 * \left(1 + \frac{0.0610 * 180}{360} \right) = €1,030,500$$

A faster way to do this is to exploit the HP-12C's simple interest calculation for n < 1.

Press **STO** **EEX** once or twice to be sure that there is no "c" on the display's lower right.

Press 6.1 **i** 1000000 **PV** 180 **Enter**
360 **÷** **n** 0 **PMT** **FV** = 1,030,500

3.
$$PV = \frac{200,000}{\left(1 + \frac{0.0522 * 36}{360} \right)} = 198,961.42$$

Press 200000 **FV** 0 **PMT** 5.22 **i** 36
Enter 360 **÷** **n** **PV** = 198,961.42

4. There are two steps to getting the answer to this question:

   Step 1: Calculate the amount due at maturity.

$$FV = 10,000,000 * \left(\frac{0.0590 * 180}{360} \right) = 10,295,000$$

   Step 2: Find the Present Value 60 days from now of the value at maturity.

$$PV = \frac{10,295,000}{\left(1 + \frac{0.0610 * (180 - 60)}{360} \right)} = 10,089,839.92$$

5.
$$1,029,313 = 1,000,000 * \left(1 + y \frac{180}{360} \right)$$

$$y = \left[\frac{1,029,313}{1,000,000} - 1 \right] * \left[\frac{360}{180} \right] = 5.863\% \; SIR_{360}$$

Exercise 33 - The Mandate - continued

6.
$$PV = \frac{1,028,250}{1 + \frac{0.0647 * 120}{360}} = 1,006,542.24$$

$$Yield = \left[\frac{1,006,542.24}{1,000,000} - 1 \right] * \left[\frac{360}{30} \right] = 7.851\%$$

When interest rates declined you generated a significant capital gain.

Exercise 34 - The Pitch

1. a.   8.160%
    b.   9.308%
    c.   8.186%
    d.   8.710%
    e.   12

2.   6.6056%
          6.6602%
          7.5000%
          7.7136%
          8.1600%
          8.2432%
          8.000%

    Note that with one compounding per year the nominal rate is equal to the effective rate.

3.   6.3300%
          6.2329%
          6.1535%
          4.7926%
          4.7642%

    Note that the nominal rate is equal to the effective rate if the compounding frequency is 1, and less than the effective rate if the compounding is greater than 1.

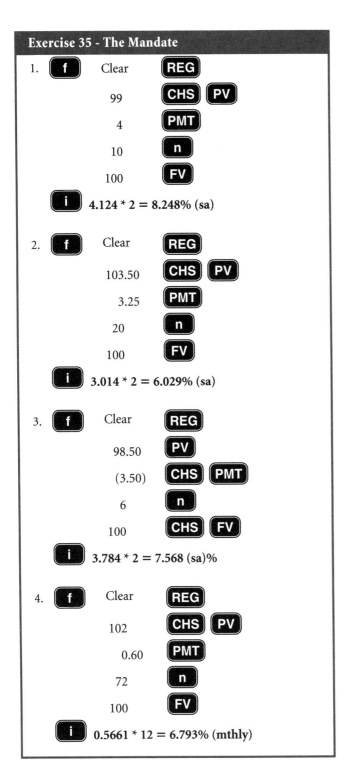

Exercise 35 - The Mandate

1. **f** Clear **REG**

   99 **CHS** **PV**

   4 **PMT**

   10 **n**

   100 **FV**

   i **4.124 * 2 = 8.248% (sa)**

2. **f** Clear **REG**

   103.50 **CHS** **PV**

   3.25 **PMT**

   20 **n**

   100 **FV**

   i **3.014 * 2 = 6.029% (sa)**

3. **f** Clear **REG**

   98.50 **PV**

   (3.50) **CHS** **PMT**

   6 **n**

   100 **CHS** **FV**

   i **3.784 * 2 = 7.568 (sa)%**

4. **f** Clear **REG**

   102 **CHS** **PV**

   0.60 **PMT**

   72 **n**

   100 **FV**

   i **0.5661 * 12 = 6.793% (mthly)**

Exercise 36 - The Pitch

1. Bond A: =   6.481%
   Bond B: =   6.218% (sa)
   To convert Bond A's yield from effective to nominal:

   f Clear **REG**

   1.06481 **Enter**

   .5 **yˣ** 1 **−**

   2 **×** **= 6.379%**

   To convert Bond B's yield from nominal to effective:

   f Clear **REG**

   .06281 **Enter**

   2 **÷** 1 **+**

   Enter **×** 1 **−** **= 6.315%**

   As a result:

	Effective	Nominal
Bond A	6.481%	6.379% (sa)
Bond B	6.315%	6.218% (sa)

   We can compare the two bonds by using either the effective column or the nominal column. In both cases Bond A has the highest yield, that is the one you should pick all other things (particularly credit) being equal. The choice of which column to use will depend on the clients' preference.

2. Bond C   7.419%
   Bond D   7.320% (sa)

	Effective	Nominal
Bond C	7.419%	7.287% (sa)
Bond D	7.454%	7.320% (sa)

   In this case choose Bond D, it has a higher YTM using either effective or nominal comparisons.

3. First calculate the other costs as a percent of par and subtract from price:
   Bond E = 101 − 1.875 − 0.04 = 99.085
   Bond F = 98 − 0.65 − 0.02 = 97.33

	Effective	Nominal
Bond E	6.973%	6.856% (sa)
Bond F	7.272%	7.144% (sa)

   Issue Bond E. It has a lower All-In-Cost.

A
N
S
W
E
R
S

Exercise 36 - The Pitch - continued

4. First calculate the other costs as a percent of par:
   Bond G = 100.50 − 2.00 − 0.04 = 98.46
   Bond H = 99 − 0.70 − 0.0333 = 98.2667

	Effective	Nominal
Bond G	7.348%	7.218% (sa)
Bond H	7.378%	7.247% (sa)

Exercise 37 - The Mandate

1. a. 7.922% (q)
   b. 7.094% (sa)
   c. 6.979% (sa)
   d. 7.092% (sa)
   e. 7.127% (q)

2. a. 6.940% (q)
   b. 6.900% (monthly)
   c. 6.881% (daily)
   d. 7.123%

Exercise 38 - The Pitch

1. 8.243%

2. 11.132%

3. 2.189% (a miserable return)

4. 7.682%

5. 5.471%

Exercise 39 - The Pitch

Calculator in M.DY date format.

1.152007 **Enter** 6.122007 **g** **ΔDYS** 117

(Act/Act) **X ↔ Y** 117 (30/360)

6.062004 **Enter** 12.062004 **g** **ΔDYS** 183

(Act/Act) **X ↔ Y** 180 (30/360)

2.152004 **Enter** 8.152004 **g** **ΔDYS** 182

(Act/Act) **X ↔ Y** 180 (30/360)

Hint: After calculating the days between dates using Actual/Actual,

press the **X ↔ Y** *key to calculate the days using 30/360.*

Exercise 40 - The Pitch

Calculator in M.DY date format.

1.042006 **Enter** 210 **g** **Date** 8,02,2006

3 = Wednesday

3.122003 **Enter** 400 **g** **Date** 4,15,2004

4 = Thursday

6.182004 **Enter** 180 **CHS** **g** **Date**

12,21,2003 7 = Sunday

Exercise 41 - The Mandate

6.50 **PMT** 6.02 **i** 10.152003 **Enter** 8.152007 **f** **Price** 101.611 **X ↔ Y** 1.077 **+**

102.689

The price (clean price) is 101.611. The accrued interest is 1.077 and the amount you must pay to buy the bond (the present value, also called the dirty price) is 102.689.

5.375 **PMT** 4.80 **i** 10.152003 **Enter** 2.152031 **f** **Price** 108.696 **X ↔ Y** 0.891 **+** 109.587

14 **PMT** 5.10 **i** 10.152003 **Enter** 11.152011 **f** **Price** 158.351 **X ↔ Y** 5.821 **+**

164.171

Exercise 42 - The Mandate

6.50 **PMT** 99.50 **PV** 10.152003 **Enter** 8.152007 **f** **YTM** 6.65%

5.375 **PMT** 96 **PV** 10.152003 **Enter** 2.152031 **f** **YTM** 5.66%

14 **PMT** 140.75 **PV** 10.152003 **Enter** 11.152011 **f** **YTM** 7.25%

Hints: 1) When calculating the yield to maturity of a bond, use the clean price. 2) If you are doing several problems using the same date, store (STO) the date and recall (RCL) it when you need it.

Exercise 43 - The Pitch

1. Use the equation

$$PV = \frac{CF_1}{i - g},$$

So

$$PV = \frac{€120}{0.10 - 0.05} = €2,400.$$

2. $$PV = \frac{AUS150,000}{0.0895 - 0.375} = AUS2,884,165.38.$$

3. $$PV = \frac{CDN20,000,000}{0.0975 - 0.0290} = CDN291,970,802.92.$$

4. **Step 1:** Find the Present Value as of the end of year 2:

$$PV_2 = \frac{CF_3}{i - g} = \frac{100}{0.10 - 0.04} = 1,666.67$$

Step 2: Find the Present Value today of the value you found in step 1. You can use the TVM keys:

f Clear **REG**

1,666.67 **PV**

0 **PMT**

2 **n**

10 **i**

PV = (1,377.41)

Notice that the first cash flow of the infinite series occurs at the end of year 3, but the Present Value of these is as of the beginning of year 3 which we label the end of year 2.

Exercise 44 - The Mandate

1.
$$PV_0 = \frac{CF_1}{i - g} = \frac{2,000}{0.125 - 0.031} = 21,276.60$$

2. **Step 1:**
$$PV_{10} = \frac{CF_{11}}{i - g} = \frac{250}{0.1060 - 0.0250} = 3,086.42$$

Step 2: Find the Present Value today:
Use the TVM keys:

f	Clear	**REG**	
	3,086.42	**FV**	
	0	**PMT**	
	10	**n**	
	10.60	**i**	

PV = (1,126.95)

3. A declining perpetuity is a cash flow stream that mining companies face as a mine is slowly used up.

$$PV_0 = \frac{CF_1}{i - g} = \frac{100}{0.1100 - -0.05} = \frac{100}{0.16} = 625$$

4. **Step 1:** Find the Present Value of the infinite series of cash flows.

$$PV_2 = \frac{CF_3}{i - g} = \frac{100}{0.093 - 0.050} = 2,325.58$$

Step 2: Find the PV_0 for the following cash flows:

Time	Cash flow
0	(1,000)
1	(500)
2	2,375.58

Use the cash flow keys: NPV = PV_0 = 531.06.

Note that you have two choices about the year to apply the constant percentage growth formula. Either year 3 (as we did in the solution), or year 4. There is no harm in using year 4. It just takes a little more work to arrive at the same answer.

Exercise 44 - continued

5. **Step 1:** Calculate

$$PV_1 = \frac{CF_2}{i - g} = \frac{21,000}{0.09 - 0.03} = 350,000,$$

Step 2: Use the cash flow keys to calculate the Present Value today, PV_0 for the following cash flows:

Time	Cash flow
0	(500,000)
1	360,000

NPV (9.00%) = (169,724.77), not a very good investment.

6. We know from the answer to question 5 that 9.00% results in a large negative NPV. We want an interest rate that results in an NPV equal to zero, so our answer is going to be considerably less than 9.00%. Set up the following table:

Rate	PV	NPV
9.00%	350,000	(169,725)
8.00%	398,148	(101,852)
6.00%	700,000	169,811
7.00%	525,000	0

So 7.00% is the IRR of the investment since it makes the NPV = 0.

Exercise 45, Solve Them!

1.	88
2.	59
3.	49
4.	1152
5.	128
6.	41

Exercise 46, Symbols in Equations

1.	41
2.	81
3.	149
4.	289

Exercise 47, Exponential

1. $a * a * a * a = a^4$
   $1.10 * 1.10 * 1.10 * 1.10 = 1.10^4 = 1.4641$

2. $c * c * c * c * c = c^5$
   $1.05^5 = 1.2763$

3. $\dfrac{1}{(1.10)^3} = 0.751$

4. $d^2 + e^3 = 2^2 + 3^3 = 4 + 27 = 0.14815$

5. $\left(\dfrac{1+g}{1+i}\right)^3 = \left(\dfrac{1.05}{1.09}\right)^3 = 0.89390$

Exercise 48, Simplify Me

1. x^7; $2^7 = 128$
2. d^6; $1.045^6 = 1.3023$
3. $(1+f)^{13} = (1.01)^{13} = 1.1381$

Exercise 49, Calculate . . .

1. a^6
2. 3.138
3. 1.629

Exercise 50, Simplify and Evaluate

1. $a^{-11} = \dfrac{1}{a^n} = \dfrac{1}{2^{11}} = 0.0004883$

2. $a^{-3} = \dfrac{1}{1.05^3} = 0.8638$

3. $\dfrac{1}{(1+f)^2} = (1+f)^{-2} = \dfrac{1}{(1.01)^2} = 0.980$

Exercise 51, More Simplify and Evaluate

1. $16^{\frac{1}{2}} = \sqrt{16} = 4$

2. $x = 3$

3. $x^{\frac{7}{12}} = 1.09^{\frac{7}{12}} = 1.0516$

   Hint: 1.09 *7* *12* ÷ y^x
   5 1.0516

Exercise 52, Solve Them

1. First subtract $4z$ from both sides
   $2z + 9 = 26$
   Next, subtract 9 from both sides
   $2z = 17$
   Finally, divide both sides by 2
   $z = 17 \div 2 = 8.5$

2. First distribute the 2
   $12w + 6y = 10w + 16$
   Next subtract $6y$ and $10w$ from both sides
   $2w = 16 - 6y$
   Finally divide by 2
   $w = 8 - 3y$

3. First add x to both sides and collect terms to get
   $4x + 3y = y^2$
   Then subtract $3y$ from both sides
   $4x = y^2 - 3y$
   Finally, divide both sides by 4
   $x = \dfrac{y^2 - 3y}{4}$

Exercise 53, Distribute!

1. $13x + 39y$
2. $x^2 + 3xy + xz$
3. $2x + 2y + 3xz + 3yz$

Exercise 54, Factor!

1. $20(a + 2b)$

2. $2xy(x + 4)$

3. $\frac{1}{2}c(d + k + 2)$

Exercise 55, Solve, Solve, Solve . . .

1. Multiply both sides by $(k - g)$, resulting in

   $(k - g) * PV = CF_1$

   Distribute out $(k - g) * PV$

   $k * PV - g * PV = CF_1$

   Add g * PV to both sides

   $k * PV = CF_1 + g * PV$

   Divide both sides by PV

   $$\frac{k*PV}{PV} = \frac{CF_1}{PV} + \frac{g*PV}{PV}$$

   And, since $\frac{PV}{PV} = 1$,

   $$k = \frac{CF_1}{PV} + g$$

   Shortcut
   When you are proficient at these algebraic manipulations you sometimes do the following in step 3:

   "move -g * PV from the left side of the equal sign to the right side and change it from negative to positive," i.e.

   From $\qquad k * PV - g * PV = CF_1$

   To $\qquad k * PV = CF_1 + g * PV$

2. **Step 1:** regroup the terms

   $x + xy + y^2 = 16$

   Step 2: factor out x

   $x(1 + y) + y^2 = 16$

   Step 3: subtract y^2

   $x(1 + y) = 16 - y^2$

   Step 4: divide by $(1 + y)$

   $$x = \frac{16 - y^2}{1 + y}$$

   Step 5: evaluate when $y = 3$

   $$x = \frac{16 - 9}{1 + 3} = \frac{7}{4} = 1.75$$

Exercise 55 - continued

3. **Step 1:** Move all terms involving p to the left side of the equal sign.

$4p + pk + 2pk + 3 = 30$

Step 2: Subtract 3 from both sides

$4p + pk + 2pk = 27$

Step 3: Factor out p

$p(4 + k + 2k) = 27$

Step 4: Add terms involving k

$p(4 + 3k) = 27$

Step 5: Divide both side by $(4 + 3k)$

$$p = \frac{27}{(4 + 3k)}$$

Step 6: Evaluate when $k = 2$

$$p = \frac{27}{(4 + 6)} = \frac{27}{10} = 2.7$$

Exercise 56

1. $\dfrac{10 + 2 + 6}{3} = \dfrac{18}{3} = 6$

2. $\dfrac{100}{1.1} + \dfrac{50}{1.1^2} = 90.909 + 41.322 = 132.231$

3. $\dfrac{6 + 9 + 16 + 25}{4} = 13.25$

Exercise 57

1.

$$\frac{100(1.04)^1}{(1.10)^1} + \frac{100(1.04)^2}{(1.10)^2} + \frac{100(1.04)^3}{(1.10)^3}$$

$94.545 + 89.388 + 84.513 = 268.447$

2. In this case t is the index. Split the problem up and work on the numerator (the top of the equation) first and put your work in a table:

(1)	(2)	(3)	(4)
t	CF_t	$\dfrac{CF_t}{(1 + y)^t}$	$\dfrac{t*CF_t}{(1 + y)^t}$
1	8.00	7.41	7.41
2	108.00	92.59	185.19
Total			**192.60**

Next we can work on the denominator (the bottom of the equation):

(1)	(2)	(3)
t	CF_t	$\dfrac{CF_t}{(1 + y)^t}$
1	8.00	7.41
2	108.00	92.59
Total		**100.00**

So finally we are left with:

$$D = \frac{192.59}{100.00} = 1.926$$

Congratulations! You have just calculated a Macaulay Duration of a 2-year bond selling at par.

INDEX

INDEX